British Aviatic
(1909-1980) Cat

From Taylorcraft To Bulldog - Auster Aircraft Advertisements 1936 - 1978

Compiled By David Robinson

ISBN 978-0-244-66263-9

Compilers Notes

The British Aviation Advertisements (1909-1980) series of catalogues are designed to provide a handy information source for researchers, enthusiasts and others with an interest in aviation. As such these publications are produced without narrative.

These listings also provide an interesting 'linear' method of tracing the evolution of an aviation company, manufacturing process or product line - a product development timeline if you prefer.

To add some context there is a small 'Extras' section at the end of each catalogue featuring some representative adverts from component manufacturers, contractors and third party suppliers.

All the images featured in this publication are reproduced from original and authentic source material in the Aviation Ancestry collection.

Advertisement sources & credit (Ad Ref:) appear immediately below each item. Ad Ref refers to the record number in the Aviation Ancestry master catalogue & database.

It should be noted that reference sources quoted are not necessarily exclusive. Identical adverts frequently appeared across multiple publications simultaneously, although minor variations in layout might be noted.

Some adverts in a year group may appear at first sight to be identical but closer inspection will normally reveal some subtle change of wording or emphasis.

All items in the catalogue are categorised by year and month. Identical adverts may appear under different year headings but should not be duplicated in any specified year. The absence of adverts in any given month doesn't necessarily mean that none were published as identical adverts may have been published at intervals.

It's worth noting that a surprising number of magazine issues never made it to the newsstand due to industrial disputes of one form or another.

That Great Britain was a class based society and still had significant Empire interests until after the Second World War is a matter of fact so it's no surprise that advertising content often reflected this. Occasionally some adverts may seem mildly amusing or even offensive to the modern eye but without the inclusion of such material essential historical context would be missing.

Quoted sources represent the best quality original examples or simply the first in the database. Originals may have been printed in full or part colour, unfortunately the cost of publishing these catalogues in a richer or full colour format proved to be prohibitive.

It's of interest to note that wartime and immediate post-war publications were subject to government economy restrictions often resulting in poor image quality. Magazines published to a monthly rather than a weekly cycle tended to be of better quality and these are the preferred source for inclusion into these catalogues.

Every effort has been made to produce as complete a catalogue as possible but it's inevitable that more items will surface from time to time and will be included in future revisions. For latest items the database at aviationancestry.co.uk should be consulted.

Sections	Page

Taylorcraft
1936 - 1946

Aeroplane June 3rd 1936
Ad Ref 17949

The SMART New "CUB"
FLEET

STABLE • STURDY • ECONOMICAL

PERFORMANCE

Top Speed.............87 m.p.h.
Cruising Speed........70 m.p.h.
Landing Speed.........28 m.p.h.
Climb........450 ft. 1st min.
Service ceiling.......12,000 ft.
Cruising Range......210 miles
Gliding Angle.........10 to 1
Gas Consumption....2½ gal. hr.
Oil Consumption......½ pt. hr.

Wing Span......35 ft. 2¼ in.
Length overall....22 ft. 3 in.
Height overall......6 ft. 8 in.
Wing Area.........178¼ sq. ft.
Wing Loading....5·44 lbs. sq. ft.
Fuel Capacity.......7½ gallons
Oil Capacity.........4 quarts

Weight empty........563 lbs.
Useful Load.........407 lbs.
Pay Load.............175 lbs.
Gross Weight........970 lbs.
Power Loading........25·5 lbs.

Delivery - THREE WEEKS

A. J. WALTER
23, ST. PETERSBURG PLACE,
LONDON, W.2
Telephone - BAYSWATER 0311

BEAUTY — COMFORT — FINER PERFORMANCE

The outstanding achievement in 1936 is the new J-2 "CUB." The Safety, economy and performance of the old "CUB" is known the world over. And now comes a smart, fleet NEW "CUB" that sets a new high in airplane value . . . value that is built into every detail . . . value that is apparent.

Added to the "CUB" that made sales history in 1935 are many improvements . . . new beauty, greater comfort and finer performance. For the past two years Taylor Aircraft Co. engineers have been developing and testing the many refinements that combine to make the new 1936 "CUB" a perfectly balanced airplane.

Don't buy ANY airplane until you see and fly the New "CUB." It's the plane you've been waiting for. The price is the same as for the old "CUB".................. **£498**

Taylorcraft 1936 - 1946

The Taylor "Cub"

FIRST :
Portsmouth Air Trophy Race

SECOND:

Shoreham and Back Race

AT

PORTSMOUTH AIR PORT

Sat. July 18th, 1936

PERFORMANCE

Top Speed	87 m.p.h.
Cruising Speed	70 m.p.h.
Landing Speed	28 m.p.h.
Climb	450 ft. 1st min.
Service Ceiling	12,000 ft.
Cruising Range	210 miles
Gliding Angle	10 to 1
Gas Consumption	2½ gal. hr.
Oil Consumption	¼ pt. hr.
Wing Span	35 ft. 2¼ in.
Length overall	22 ft. 5 in.
Height overall	6ft. 8 in.
Wing Area	178¾ sq. ft.
Wing Loading	5.44 lbs. sq. ft.
Fuel Capacity	7½ gallons
Oil Capacity	4 quarts

FITTED WITH "SERVAIS" SILENCER

Added to the CUB that made sales history in 1935 are many improvements . . new beauty, greater comfort and finer performance. For the past two years Taylor Aircraft Co. engineers have been developing and testing the many refinements that combine to make the new 1936 CUB a perfectly balanced airplane. Don't buy ANY airplane until you see and fly the New "CUB." It's the plane you've been waiting for. Delivery Three Weeks.

£498

A. J. WALTER, Tollerton Airport

NOTTINGHAM

Telephone: PLUMTREE 14

Aeropilot August 1936
Ad Ref 17955

8

Taylorcraft 1936 - 1946

Aeroplane August 26th 1936
Ad Ref 17954

9

Aeroplane December 2nd 1936
Ad Ref 17953

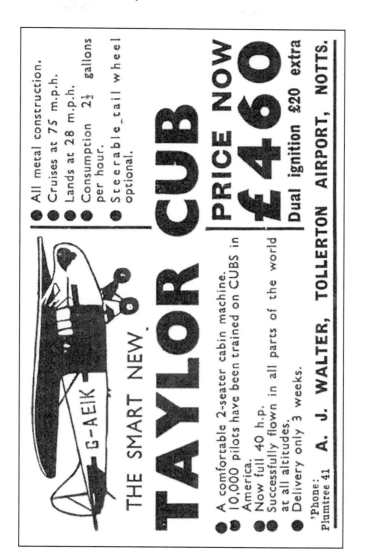

Aeroplane December 9th 1936
Ad Ref 17952

Aeroplane December 16th 1936
Ad Ref 17951

Aeroplane March 3rd 1937
Ad Ref 19597

Taylorcraft 1936 - 1946

Aeroplane March 10th 1937
Ad Ref 19593

14

Aeroplane April 7th 1937
Ad Ref 19598

Aeroplane April 21st 1937
Ad Ref 19596

Aeroplane May 12th 1937
Ad Ref 19594

Taylorcraft 1936 - 1946

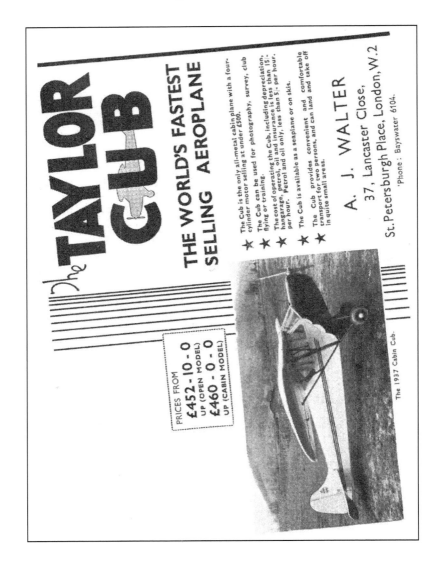

Aeroplane June 23rd 1937
Ad Ref 19595

18

Aeroplane June 30th 1937
Ad Ref 19591

Taylorcraft 1936 - 1946

Popular Flying July 1937
Ad Ref 19592

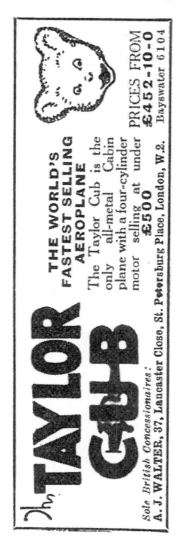

Aeroplane January 12th 1938
Ad Ref 21061

Taylorcraft 1936 - 1946

The New Silver CUB

THE WORLD'S FASTEST SELLING AIRPLANE

Here's a Plane that *You* can own!

★ The Cub is the only all-metal cabin plane with a four-cylinder motor selling at under £500.

★ The Cub can be used for photography, survey, club flying or training.

★ The cost of operating the Cub, including depreciation, hangarage, petrol, oil and insurance is less than 15/- per hour. Petrol and oil only, less than 5/- per hour.

★ The Cub is available as a seaplane or on skiis.

★ The Cub provides convenient and comfortable transport for two persons, and can land and take off in quite small areas. Write for descriptive folder.

A. J. WALTER

37, Lancaster Close,
St. Petersburgh Place, London, W.2

Bayswater 6104.

PRICES FROM
£452 - 10 - 0

Aeroplane March 9th 1938
Ad Ref 21063

Flight March 17th 1938
Ad Ref 21062

Aeroplane April 6th 1938
Ad Ref 21064

Aeroplane April 27th 1938
Ad Ref 21065

Aeroplane November 30th 1938
Ad Ref 21066

45 minutes to the Sea

● Any Taylorcraft Plus club member can fly 100 miles in the hour in comfort and warmth.

● His Club is never more than an hour from the sea, and rarely more than 40 minutes, and what interesting minutes they are.

● He can enjoy the company of the comrade at his side, conversing quietly on the countryside they look down on.

● Soon every town on the coast and inland will have its landing ground, and Taylorcraft will encourage the "A" licensed pilot to visit them.

● In the meantime, it is the most modern trainer — fully aerobatic, British made.

● Comprehensive Insurance at the lowest rate ever offered because, in the opinion of the Underwriters, it is the strongest and safest trainer yet made.

TAYLORCRAFT AEROPLANES (ENGLAND) LTD.
BRITANNIA WORKS, THURMASTON, LEICESTER
Telegrams: "Taycraft, Leicester." Telephone: Syston 85219

"LET US GO SOUTH TOGETHER"

Aeroplane March 8th 1939
Ad Ref 60428

Flight April 20th 1939
Ad Ref 21873

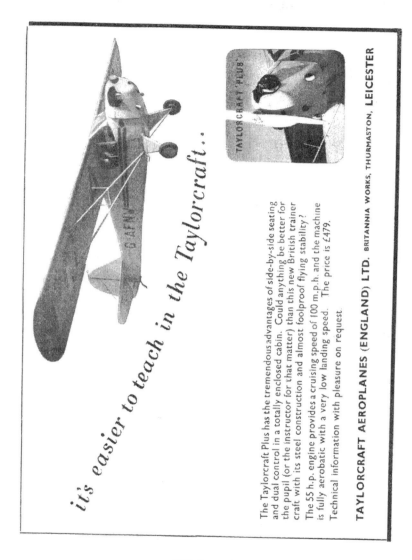

it's easier to teach in the Taylorcraft...

TAYLORCRAFT 'PLUS'

The Taylorcraft Plus has the tremendous advantages of side-by-side seating and dual control in a totally enclosed cabin. Could anything be better for the pupil (or the instructor for that matter) than this new British trainer craft with its steel construction and almost foolproof flying stability?

The 55 h.p. engine provides a cruising speed of 100 m.p.h. and the machine is fully aerobatic with a very low landing speed. The price is £479. Technical information with pleasure on request.

TAYLORCRAFT AEROPLANES (ENGLAND) LTD. BRITANNIA WORKS, THURMASTON, LEICESTER

Flight July 13th 1939
Ad Ref 21872

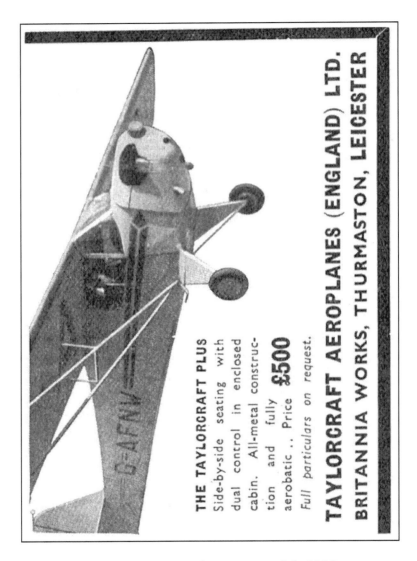

Aeroplane August 9th 1939
Ad Ref 21870

Flight August 31st 1939
Ad Ref 21871

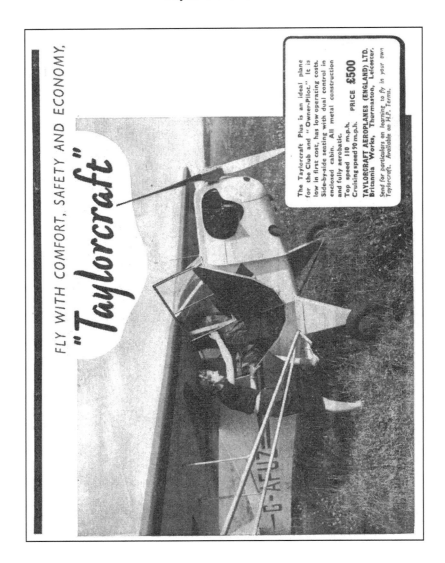

Flight September 7th 1939
Ad Ref 21874

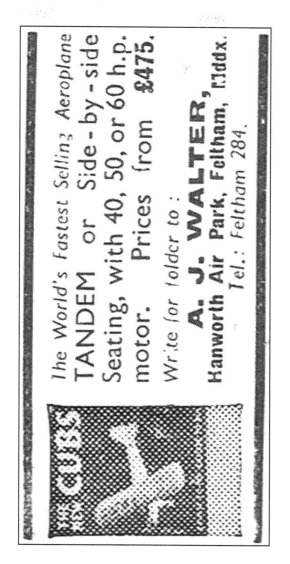

The World's Fastest Selling Aeroplane

TANDEM or Side-by-side Seating, with 40, 50, or 60 h.p. motor. Prices from **£475.**

Write for folder to :

A. J. WALTER, Hanworth Air Park, Feltham, Mddx.

Tel.: Feltham 284.

Flight January 4th 1940
Ad Ref 23860

Taylorcraft 1936 - 1946

Flight December 11th 1941
Ad Ref 25627

Aeroplane January 30th 1942
Ad Ref 25632

Taylorcraft 1936 - 1946

Aeroplane February 27th 1942
Ad Ref 25630

Flight March 12th 1942
Ad Ref 25631

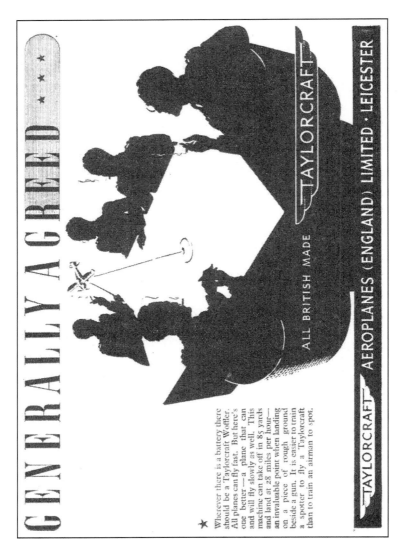

Flight April 9th 1942
Ad Ref 25629

Aeroplane May 15th 1942
Ad Ref 25637

Aeroplane June 26th 1942
Ad Ref 25638

Taylorcraft 1936 - 1946

Flight July 2nd 1942
Ad Ref 25636

Taylorcraft 1936 - 1946

Aeroplane July 24th 1942
Ad Ref 25628

42

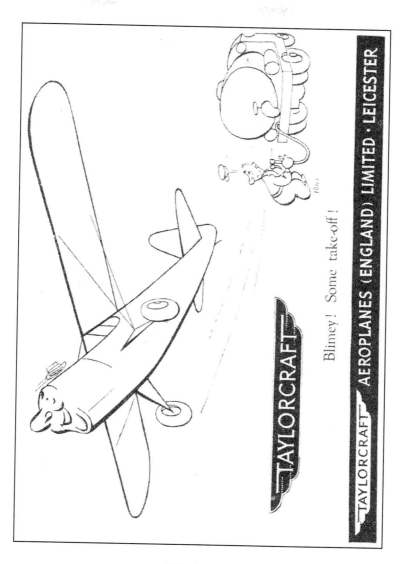

Flight July 30th 1942
Ad Ref 25639

Flight September 3rd 1942
Ad Ref 25643

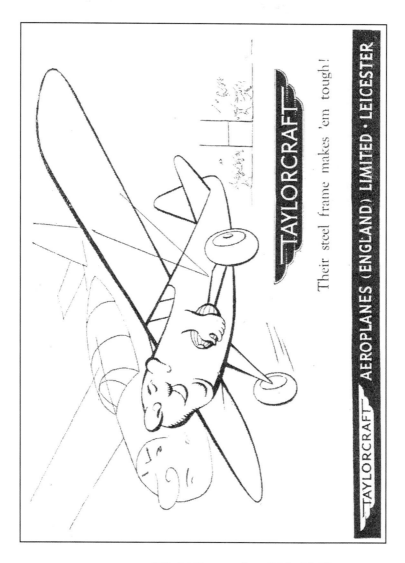

Flight September 24th 1942
Ad Ref 25641

Aeroplane October 2nd 1942
Ad Ref 25634

Flight October 22nd 1942
Ad Ref 25642

Aeroplane October 30th 1942
Ad Ref 25635

Taylorcraft 1936 - 1946

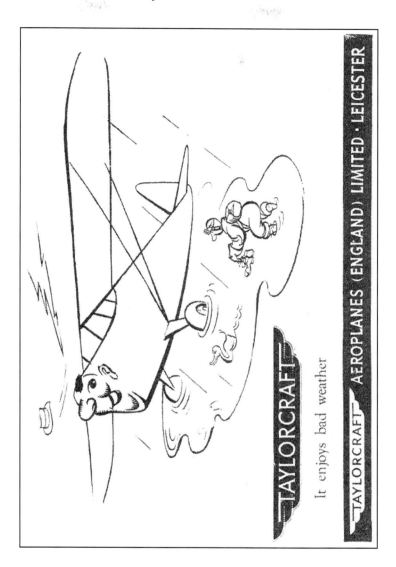

Flight November 19th 1942
Ad Ref 25640

49

Aeroplane December 4th 1942
Ad Ref 25633

Flight December 31st 1942
Ad Ref 25644

Aeroplane January 8th 1943
Ad Ref 25645

Taylorcraft 1936 - 1946

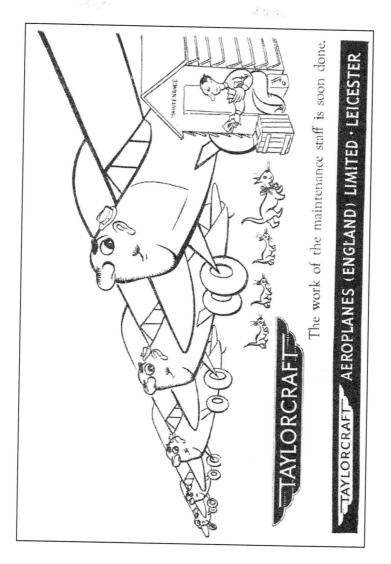

Flight January 21st 1943
Ad Ref 25654

Aeroplane February 19th 1943
Ad Ref 25650

Taylorcraft 1936 - 1946

Flight March 11th 1943
Ad Ref 25652

55

Aeroplane April 2nd 1943
Ad Ref 25648

Taylorcraft 1936 - 1946

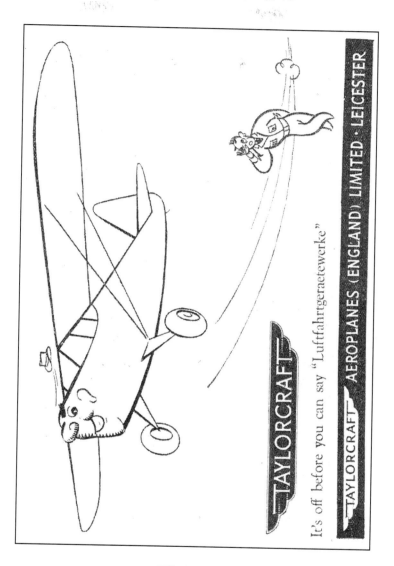

Flight April 15th 1943
Ad Ref 25653

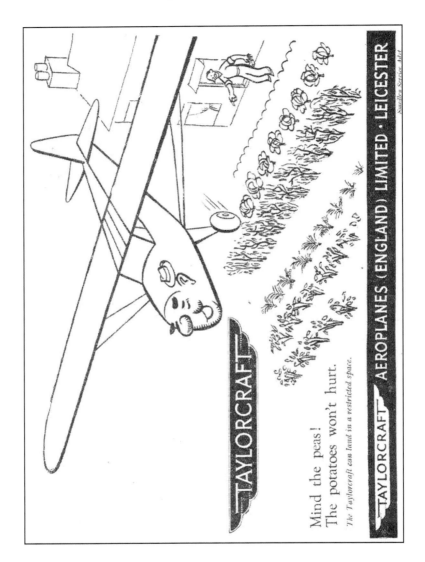

Flight June 10th 1943
Ad Ref 25656

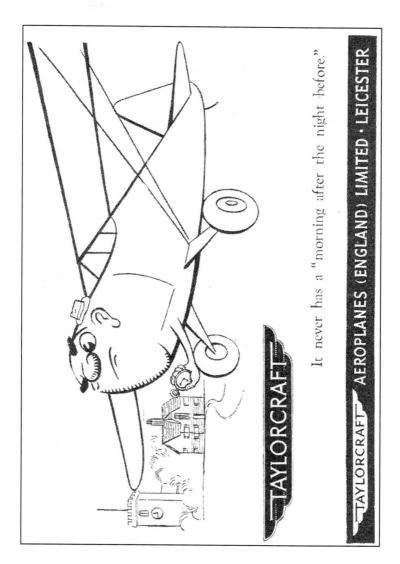

Flight July 1st 1943
Ad Ref 25655

Taylorcraft 1936 - 1946

Aeroplane August 6th 1943
Ad Ref 25651

60

Post-War Jeep

Brings flying within the reach of Young England.
Reliable and of robust construction, the Taylorcraft
solves the problem of after-the-war flying.

TAYLORCRAFT

TAYLORCRAFT AEROPLANES (England), LTD., Britannia Works, Thurmaston, LEICESTER.

Flight August 26th 1943
Ad Ref 25649

Taylorcraft 1936 - 1946

Aeroplane December 10th 1943
Ad Ref 25646

62

Flight December 30th 1943
Ad Ref 25647

Taylorcraft 1936 - 1946

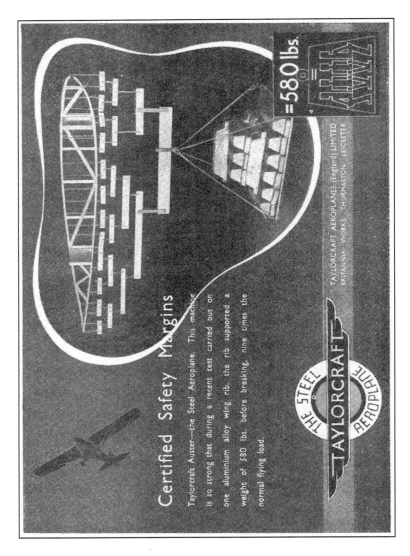

Aeroplane January 21st 1944
Ad Ref 25657

Flight February 10th 1944
Ad Ref 25658

Flight February 24th 1944
Ad Ref 25673

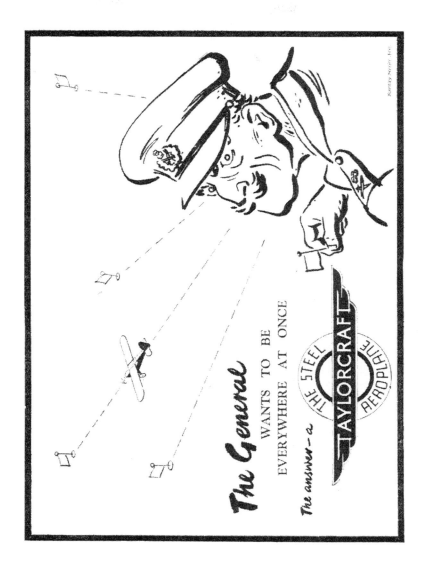

Flight March 9th 1944
Ad Ref 25667

Taylorcraft 1936 - 1946

Aeroplane March 17th 1944
Ad Ref 25668

Aeroplane April 14th 1944
Ad Ref 25666

Taylorcraft 1936 - 1946

Flight April 20th 1944
Ad Ref 25676

70

Flight May 4th 1944
Ad Ref 25665

Aeroplane June 2nd 1944
Ad Ref 25669

Taylorcraft 1936 - 1946

Aeroplane June 23rd 1944
Ad Ref 25664

73

Flight June 29th 1944
Ad Ref 25663

Taylorcraft 1936 - 1946

Aeroplane August 4th 1944
Ad Ref 25670

75

Flight August 24th 1944
Ad Ref 25662

Flight September 7th 1944
Ad Ref 25671

Aeroplane October 6th 1944
Ad Ref 25677

Flight October 19th 1944
Ad Ref 25660

Flight November 16th 1944
Ad Ref 25661

Flight November 30th 1944
Ad Ref 25672

Flight December 14th 1944
Ad Ref 25659

Taylorcraft 1936 - 1946

Flight December 28th 1944
Ad Ref 25674

Flight February 22nd 1945
Ad Ref 25695

Taylorcraft 1936 - 1946

Aeroplane March 2nd 1945
Ad Ref 25683

86

Aeroplane March 9th 1945
Ad Ref 25682

Flight April 5th 1945
Ad Ref 25684

Aeroplane April 27th 1945
Ad Ref 25685

Taylorcraft 1936 - 1946

Aeroplane May 25th 1945
Ad Ref 25686

90

Aeroplane June 8th 1945
Ad Ref 25681

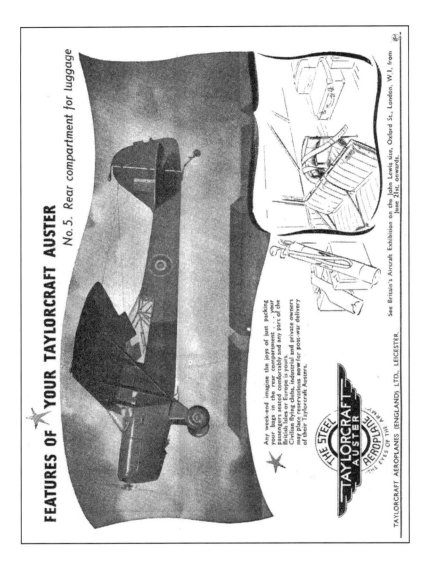

Flight June 28th 1945
Ad Ref 25687

Flight July 12th 1945
Ad Ref 25679

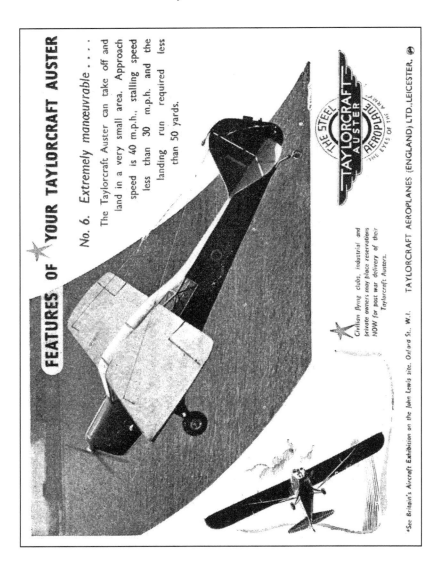

Aeroplane July 20th 1945
Ad Ref 25688

Aeroplane July 27th 1945
Ad Ref 25680

Aeroplane August 17th 1945
Ad Ref 25689

Aeroplane September 14th 1945
Ad Ref 25690

Taylorcraft 1936 - 1946

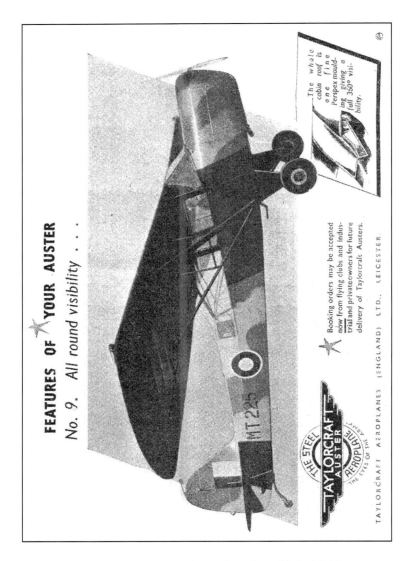

Aeroplane October 12th 1945
Ad Ref 25691

100

Flight November 15th 1945
Ad Ref 25692

✳

TAYLORCRAFT (Auster) IS THE ONLY BRITISH COMPANY WHICH HAS SUPPLIED A.O.P. AIRCRAFT IN QUANTITIES FOR BRITISH ARMY USE.

TAYLORCRAFT AEROPLANES (England) LTD., LEICESTER.

Aeroplane November 16th 1945
Ad Ref 25694

FEATURES OF YOUR AUSTER

No.11. Low running and maintenance costs

As cheap to run as a car.

Engine is very accessible for all servicing requirements.

THE STEEL TAYLORCRAFT AUSTER AEROPLANE THE EYES OF THE ARMY

TAYLORCRAFT AEROPLANES (England) LTD., LEICESTER

Flight December 13th 1945
Ad Ref 25693

Taylorcraft 1936 - 1946

Aeroplane January 4th 1946
Ad Ref 25698

Aeroplane February 1st 1946
Ad Ref 25699

Aeroplane March 1st 1946
Ad Ref 25697

Auster Aircraft

FROM THE DAY
THE PROTOTYPE
FIRST FLEW . . . .

Right from the start the Auster proved itself to be Britain's most versatile and economical light aircraft. Since its distinguished war service as the eyes of the Army, refinements have been added which further enhance its appeal to the private owner.

The Auster was the only British aircraft produced in quantity to meet the requirements of the Army for Artillery observation.

AUSTER AIRCRAFT LIMITED
REARSBY   LEICESTER

Aeroplane January 10th 1947
Ad Ref 25711

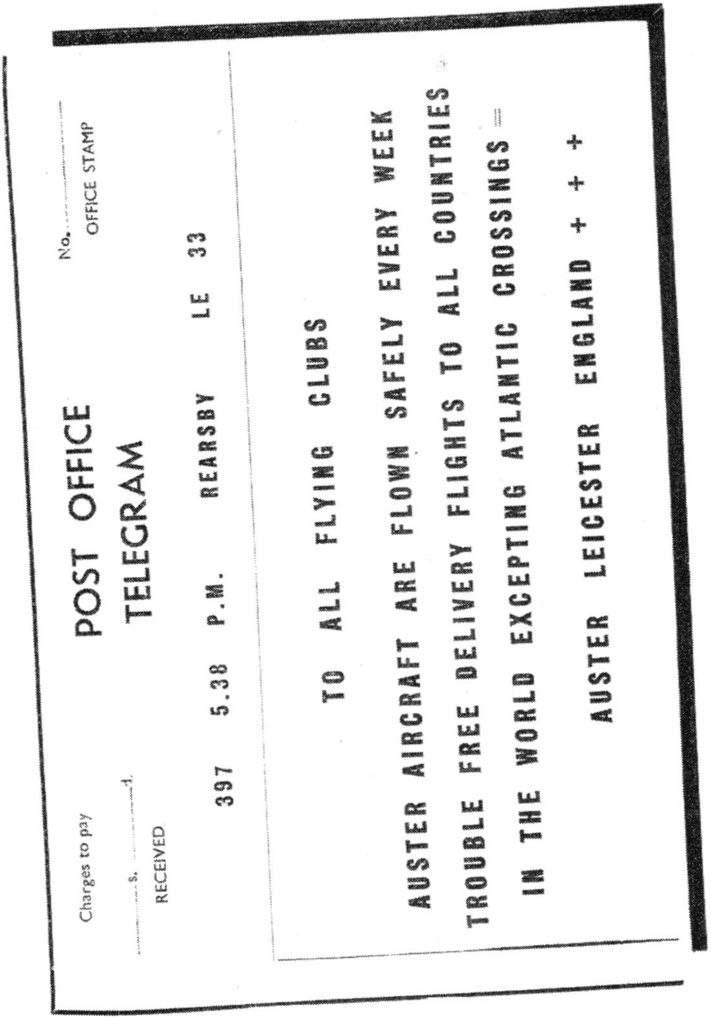

POST OFFICE
TELEGRAM

Charges to pay
s.
RECEIVED

No.
OFFICE STAMP

397   5.38 P.M.   REARSBY   LE 33

TO ALL FLYING CLUBS

AUSTER AIRCRAFT ARE FLOWN SAFELY EVERY WEEK
TROUBLE FREE DELIVERY FLIGHTS TO ALL COUNTRIES
IN THE WORLD EXCEPTING ATLANTIC CROSSINGS =

AUSTER LEICESTER ENGLAND + + +

Flight January 16th 1947
Ad Ref 25715

Flight April 3rd 1947
Ad Ref 25714

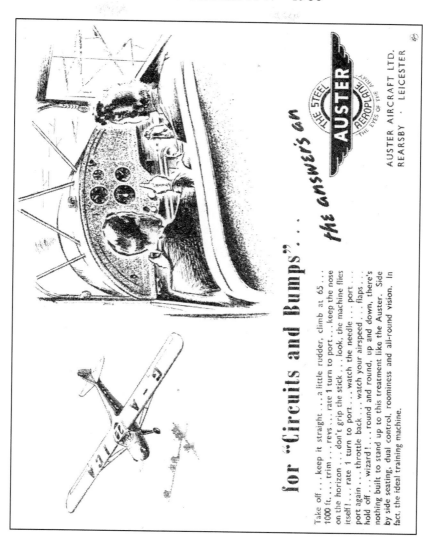

for "Circuits and Bumps"... the answer's an

AUSTER

THE STEEL AEROPLANE
THE EYES OF THE ARMY

AUSTER AIRCRAFT LTD.
REARSBY · LEICESTER

Take off . . . keep it straight . . . a little rudder, climb at 65 . . . 1000 ft., . . . trim . . . revs . . . rate 1 turn to port . . . keep the nose on the horizon . . . don't grip the stick . . . look, the machine flies itself ! . . . rate 1 turn to port . . . watch the needle . . . port . . . port again . . . throttle back . . . watch your airspeed . . . flaps . . . hold off . . . wizard ! . . . round and round, up and down, there's nothing built to stand up to this treatment like the Auster. Side by side seating, dual control, roominess and all-round vision. In fact, the ideal training machine.

Aeroplane April 18th 1947
Ad Ref 25720

Auster Aircraft Ltd.

take pleasure

in announcing that

R. K. DUNDAS LTD.

LONDON & PORTSMOUTH

have been appointed

AUSTER DISTRIBUTORS *for* *the* LONDON TERRITORY

Aeroplane May 2nd 1947
Ad Ref 25716

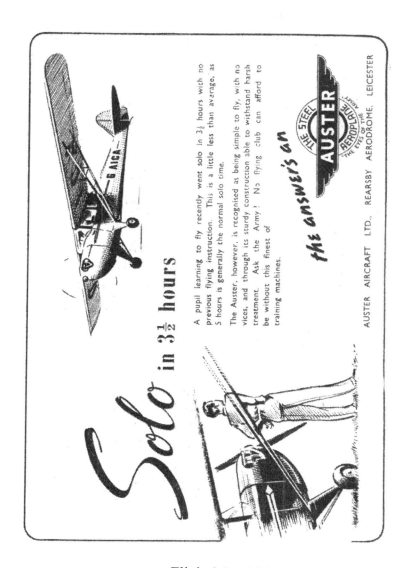

Flight May 29th 1947
Ad Ref 60471

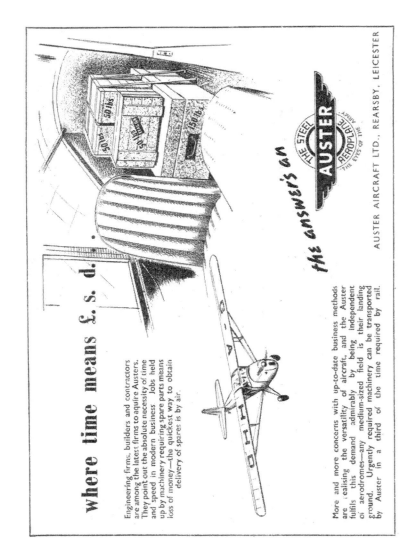

Aeroplane June 13th 1947
Ad Ref 25713

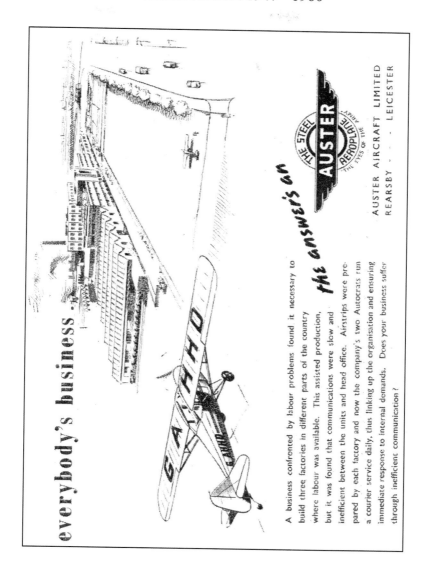

Aeroplane July 11th 1947
Ad Ref 25718

Aeroplane August 15th 1947
Ad Ref 25721

Flight September 11th 1947
Ad Ref 25719

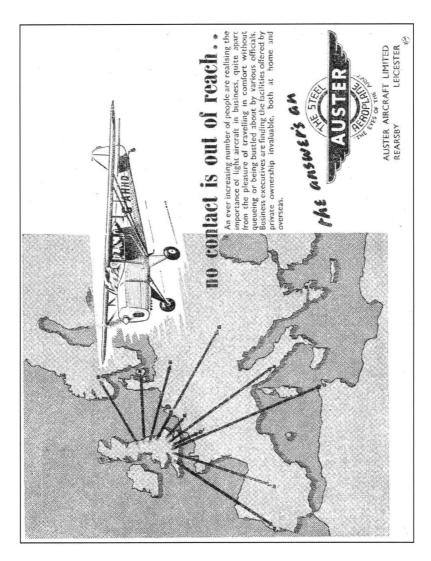

Aeroplane October 10th 1947
Ad Ref 25712

Auster Aircraft 1947 - 1960

Aeroplane November 14th 1947
Ad Ref 25717

119

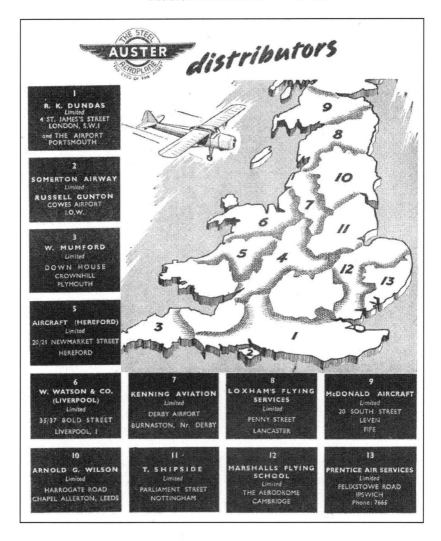

Aeroplane February 27th 1948
Ad Ref 25725

Aeroplane July 2nd 1948
Ad Ref 25723

Flight September 9th 1948
Ad Ref 25724

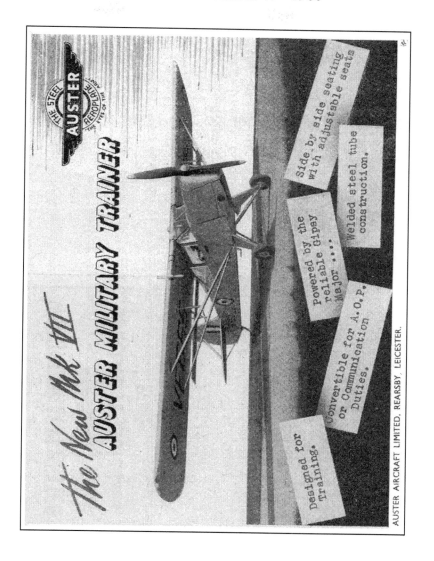

Aeroplane September 17th 1948
Ad Ref 25722

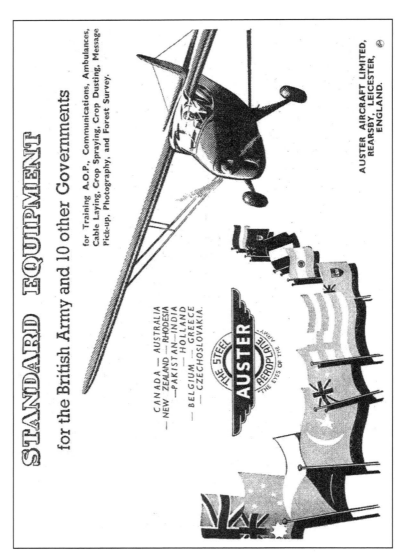

Flight April 14th 1949
Ad Ref 25726

Aeroplane June 3rd 1949
Ad Ref 25727

Auster Aircraft 1947 - 1960

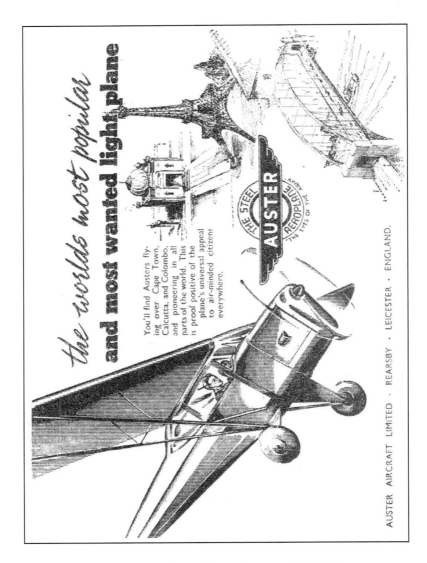

Aeroplane August 5th 1949
Ad Ref 25728

126

Aeronautics September 1949
Ad Ref 61415

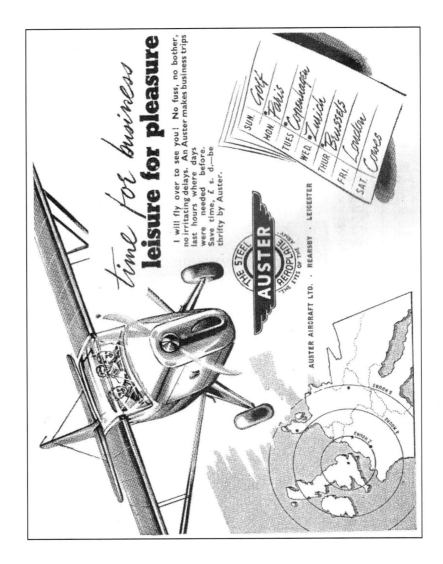

Aeronautics November 1949
Ad Ref 61416

Flight September 7th 1951
Ad Ref 29293

Aeroplane March 28th 1952
Ad Ref 30000

Aeroplane May 2nd 1952
Ad Ref 30001

Aeroplane August 29th 1952
Ad Ref 29999

Flight August 29th 1952
Ad Ref 29998

Flight May 22nd 1953
Ad Ref 31576

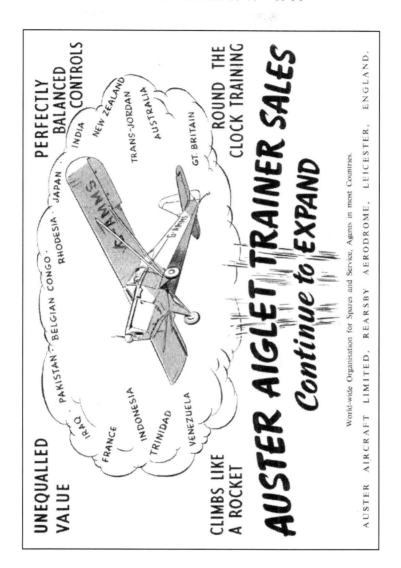

Aeroplane June 26th 1953
Ad Ref 31574

Flight July 31st 1953
Ad Ref 31575

Aeroplane September 4th 1953
Ad Ref 59784

Aeroplane March 12th 1954
Ad Ref 33515

IS NOW IN PRODUCTION FOR SERVICE

with the BRITISH ARMY

Austers have designed and built all the A.O.P. aircraft used in quantity by the British Army since 1940. The experience gained during that time has been incorporated into the Mk. 9, resulting in an aircraft *designed for the job.* Its primary function is that of a two-seat Air Observation Post, but its roomy cabin and brilliant performance well suit it to the other roles that A.O.P. aircraft are expected to perform, such as light liaison, casualty evacuation, supplies and mail dropping, aerial photography, etc., etc.

★
NEW—liquid-sprung undercarriage
NEW—cantilever metal tail unit
NEW—bigger, more powerful flaps
NEW—three doors to cabin
NEW—more comfortable cockpit

S.B.A.C. SHOW
STAND NUMBER 165

AUSTER AIRCRAFT LIMITED, REARSBY AERODROME,
LEICESTERSHIRE

Telegrams: "Auster, Leicester."   *Telephone: Rearsby 321.*

Aeroplane September 10th 1954
Ad Ref 33516

Auster Aircraft 1947 - 1960

Aeroplane January 28th 1955
Ad Ref 35061

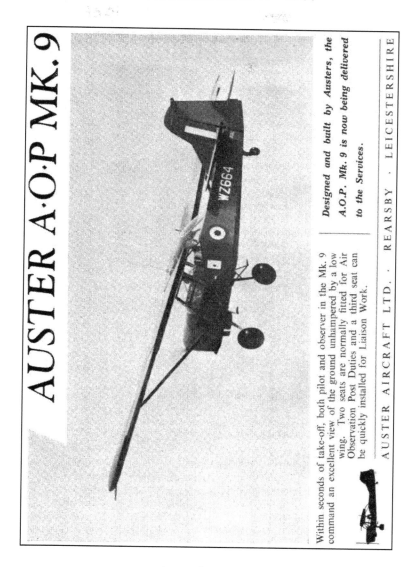

AUSTER A·O·P MK. 9

Within seconds of take-off, both pilot and observer in the Mk. 9 command an excellent view of the ground unhampered by a low wing. Two seats are normally fitted for Air Observation Post Duties and a third seat can be quickly installed for Liaison Work.

Designed and built by Austers, the A.O.P. Mk. 9 is now being delivered to the Services.

AUSTER AIRCRAFT LTD. · REARSBY · LEICESTERSHIRE

Aeroplane March 4th 1955
Ad Ref 35062

141

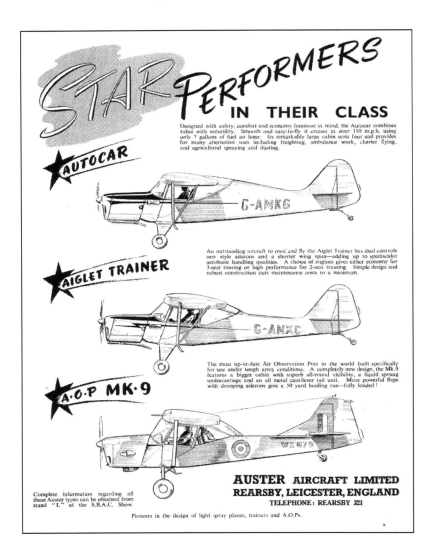

Aeroplane September 9th 1955
Ad Ref 35063

The Aeroplane August 31st 1956
Ad Ref 3076

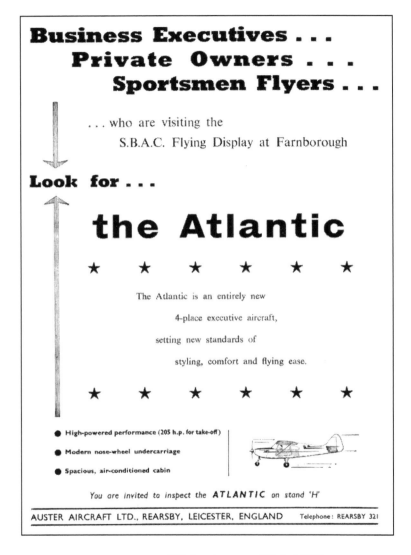
Flight August 30th 1957
Ad Ref 38343

Flight March 25th 1960
Ad Ref 39387

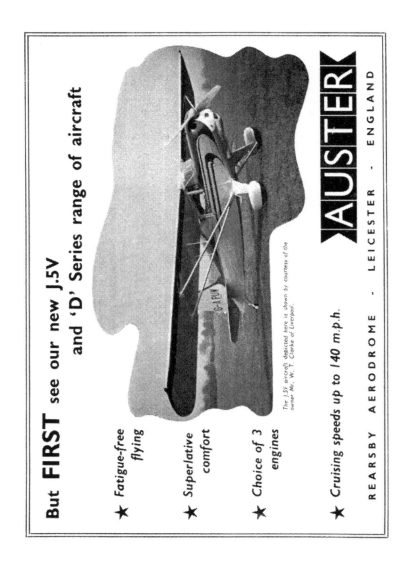

Aeroplane May 20th 1960
Ad Ref 39385

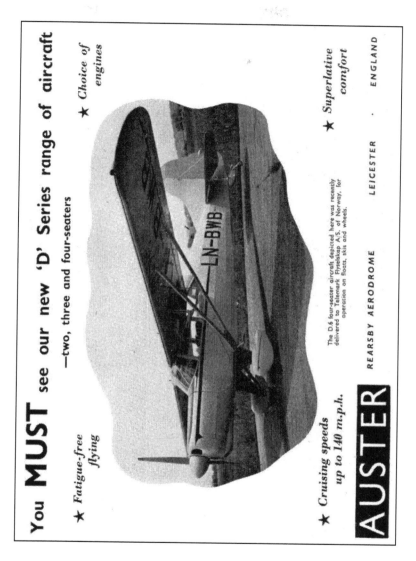

Flight September 2nd 1960
Ad Ref 39388

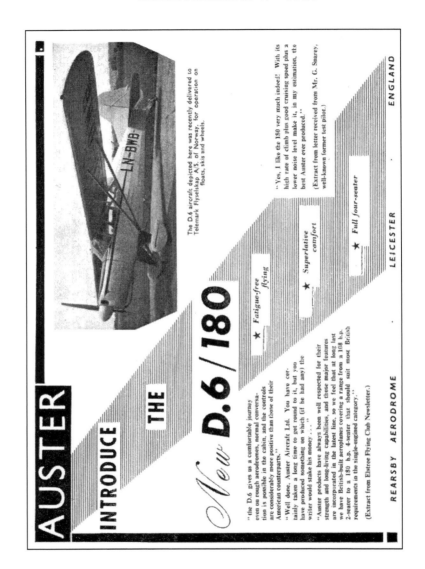

Aeroplane September 9th 1960
Ad Ref 39386

Beagle Aircraft

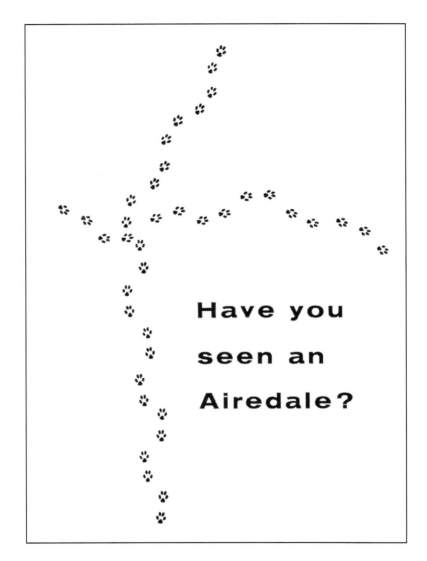

Aeroplane April 20th 1961
Ad Ref 60860

"Don't look now! but there's an **AIREDALE** coming"

Flight April 20th 1961
Ad Ref 15078

Flight April 27th 1961
Ad Ref 15076

Air Pictorial June 1961
Ad Ref 4324

Order of Excellence?

What are the qualities that a buyer looks for in a
light executive/touring aeroplane? Reliability, comfort, economy,
performance, good looks? And in what order?

Whichever way you look at the new BEAGLE AIREDALE it scores well.
It is comfortable, quiet and has good furnishings; it has a rugged airframe
and a dependable engine. It has all-weather equipment for day and
night flying. It is inexpensive to buy and it is attractively cheap to operate.
It has a vivid performance with outstanding range capability. And it is elegant.
The AIREDALE is good business—and it is British.

QUALITY — PERFORMANCE — ECONOMY

BEAGLE-Auster Aircraft Ltd

Rearsby Aerodrome, Rearsby, Leicester, England. Telephone: Rearsby 321.

 BRITISH EXECUTIVE AND GENERAL AVIATION LIMITED   BUY BEAGLE — BUY BRITISH

Flight June 29th 1961
Ad Ref 15083

Report on Airedale

PHOTOGRAPH BY COURTESY OF "THE AEROPLANE & ASTRONAUTICS"

The BEAGLE Airedale is the new British, four seat, light executive aircraft and it will soon be in service.

On the 16th April an Airedale flew for the first time.

On the 24th May the Provisional Certificate of Airworthiness was received. Tests are now being completed for the issue by the Air Registration Board of Full Transport Category Certification—including tropical clearance. The first aircraft is completing its tests for the semi-aerobatic category, including spins.

By the 30th September ten Airedales will have been completed; production will then be at the rate of three a week.

Handling qualities and performance are both better than our original estimates, and so are sales. We are pleased with the Airedale and we believe that you will be.

The Airedale is good business—and it is British.

BEAGLE-Auster Aircraft Limited

Aerodromes at Shoreham, Rearsby and Kidlington.

 BRITISH EXECUTIVE AND GENERAL AVIATION LIMITED

Sceptre House, Regent Street, London, W.1.

Flight August 3rd 1961
Ad Ref 15081

The first
BEAGLE twin
POWERED BY ROLLS-ROYCE

British Executive and General Aviation Limited are proud to announce their first twin engine luxury executive aircraft the BEAGLE B.206. This five/seven seat aircraft will be on show for the first time at Farnborough, see it on Stand G from 3rd September.

BRITISH EXECUTIVE AND GENERAL AVIATION LIMITED

Sceptre House, Regent Street, London, W.1. Telephone: Regent 3101-5

 · AERODROMES AT SHOREHAM, REARSBY AND KIDLINGTON

Air Pictorial September 1961
Ad Ref 4334

Aeroplane September 7th 1961
Ad Ref 15080

Flight October 5th 1961
Ad Ref 15077

Symbol of progress

A boost for business from BEAGLE. The speed with which BEAGLE has introduced a new range of light executive aircraft has captured the imagination of the aviation and business worlds. BEAGLE aircraft are a symbol of progress and modern thinking in national and international commerce.

British Executive and General Aviation Limited
Sceptre House, Regent Street, London, W.1. Telephone: Regent 3101-5

Aerodromes at Shoreham, Rearsby and Kidlington

Aeroplane December 7th 1961
Ad Ref 15079

Aeroplane December 21st 1961
Ad Ref 60861

Beagle Aircraft 1960 - 1969

Aeroplane February 15th 1962
Ad Ref 60908

161

Flight February 22nd 1962
Ad Ref 39712

(Photograph: British Travel and Holidays Association)

135

minutes Manchester - Inverness by Airedale

The Airedale—first of the BEAGLE range—a four-seat private and executive aeroplane which takes such journeys in its stride. The Airedale brings winter sports to your door step. A weekend's ski-ing in Scotland without the fuss and bother of tedious arrangements. The exceptional flying qualities and ease of control makes the Airedale a pilot's aeroplane unequalled in its class; handling is docile but precise, and landing under all conditions extremely easy. The Airedale is the ideal beginner's plane and inspires confidence right from the start.

BRITISH EXECUTIVE AND GENERAL AVIATION LIMITED
SCEPTRE HOUSE, REGENT STREET, LONDON, W.1   TELEPHONE REGENT 3101-5
Aerodromes at Shoreham, Rearsby and Kidlington

Air Pictorial April 1962
Ad Ref 4139

Photograph British Travel and Holidays Association.

125 minutes Birmingham – Lands End by Airedale

The Airedale—first of the BEAGLE range—a four-seat private and executive aeroplane—enables you to travel from city centre to seashore in speed and comfort. The Airedale brings the pleasures of swimming, surf riding and boating within your reach not just once or twice but a dozen times or more a year. The exceptional flying qualities and ease of control make the Airedale a pilot's aeroplane unequalled in its class; handling is docile but precise, and landing under all conditions extremely easy. The Airedale is the ideal beginners plane and inspires confidence right from the start.

BEAGLE **BRITISH EXECUTIVE AND GENERAL AVIATION LIMITED**
Sceptre House, Regent Street, London, W.1. Telephone: Regent 3101-5
Aerodromes at Shoreham, Rearsby and Kidlington.

Flight April 5th 1962
Ad Ref 51217

Beagle Aircraft 1960 - 1969

HOW **many minutes to Sywell?**

Not many by Airedale—first of the BEAGLE range—a four-seat private and executive aeroplane which brings such events as Shackleton International Aircraft Display to your door step. Visit Sywell (Northampton) Airport on 13th, 14th and 15th of April and see the BEAGLE stand. Here you will find a vivid presentation of the BEAGLE range of aircraft and flying demonstrations of the Airedale, and the Terrier 2—a high-performance low-cost training touring aircraft. Take this opportunity to find out more about the exciting development in light aviation engineered by BEAGLE. BUY BEAGLE.... FLY BRITISH

BEAGLE AIRCRAFT LIMITED
Sceptre House, Regent Street, London, W.1. Telephone: Regent 3181 5
Aerodromes at SHOREHAM, REARSBY and KIDLINGTON.

Flight April 12th 1962
Ad Ref 51218

TWO of the BEAGLE range available now

The **BEAGLE-Auster Airedale.** (TOP) A four-seat private and executive aircraft powered by a Lycoming 180 b.h.p. engine. **Price: £5,500** (FULLY EQUIPPED LESS RADIO)

The **BEAGLE-Auster Terrier 2.** (BOTTOM) A sturdy two/three seat aircraft ideal for training, touring or club use, powered by a 140 b.h.p. de Havilland Gipsy Major engine. **Price: £2,195.**

BEAGLE AIRCRAFT LIMITED
Sceptre House, Regent Street, London W.1. Telephone: Regent 3101-5
Aerodromes at Shoreham, Rearsby and Kidlington

Flight April 19th 1962
Ad Ref 39713

Flight May 10th 1962
Ad Ref 51219

110 minutes London—Le Mans by Airedale

The Airedale – first of the BEAGLE range – a four seat private and executive aeroplane which takes such journeys in its stride. The Airedale brings such international events as the famous Le Mans 24 hour race to your doorstep. International sport made local without the fuss and bother of tedious arrangements. The exceptional flying qualities and ease of control makes the Airedale a pilot's aeroplane unequalled in its class; handling is docile but precise, and landing under all conditions extremely easy. The Airedale is the ideal beginner's plane and inspires confidence right from the start.

BEAGLE AIRCRAFT LIMITED
Sceptre House, Regent Street, London, W.1. Telephone : Regent 3101/5
Aerodromes at SHOREHAM, REARSBY and KIDLINGTON.

Flight May 31st 1962
Ad Ref 39710

Flight July 5th 1962
Ad Ref 39711

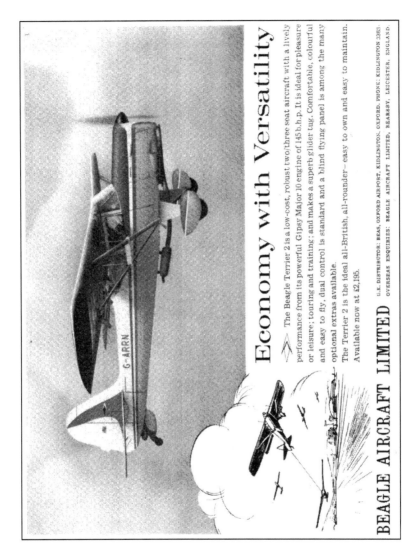

Flight August 2nd 1962
Ad Ref 39714

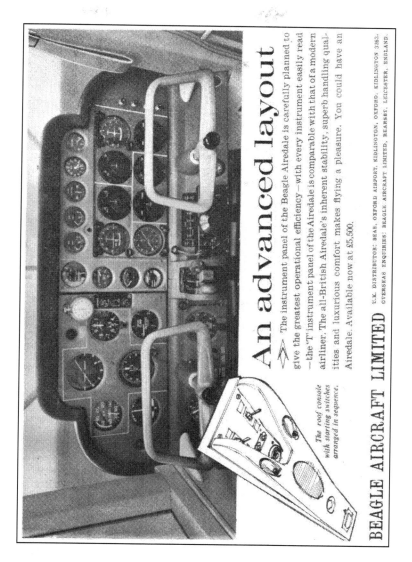

An advanced layout

→ The instrument panel of the Beagle Airedale is carefully planned to give the greatest operational efficiency — with every instrument easily read — the 'T' instrument panel of the Airedale is comparable with that of a modern airliner. The all-British Airedale's inherent stability, superb handling qualities and luxurious comfort makes flying a pleasure. You could have an Airedale. Available now at £5,500.

BEAGLE AIRCRAFT LIMITED

U.K. DISTRIBUTOR: BEAS, OXFORD AIRPORT, KIDLINGTON, OXFORD. KIDLINGTON 3383. OVERSEAS ENQUIRIES: BEAGLE AIRCRAFT LIMITED, REARSBY, LEICESTER, ENGLAND.

The roof console with starting switches arranged in sequence.

Flight August 16th 1962
Ad Ref 39715

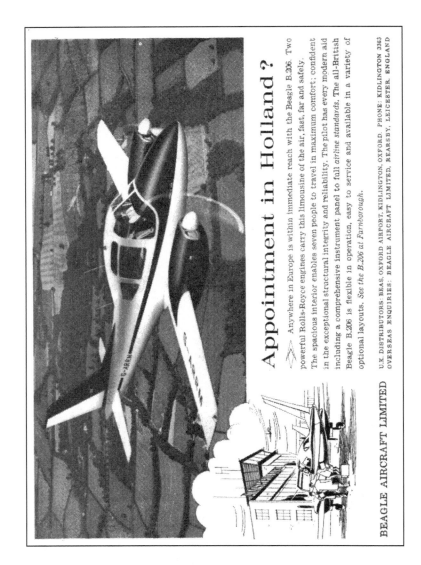

Appointment in Holland ?

Anywhere in Europe is within immediate reach with the Beagle B.206. Two powerful Rolls-Royce engines carry this limousine of the air, fast, far and safely. The spacious interior enables seven people to travel in maximum comfort; confident in the exceptional structural integrity and reliability. The pilot has every modern aid including a comprehensive instrument panel to full *airline standards*. The all-British Beagle B.206 is flexible in operation, easy to service and available in a variety of optional layouts. *See the B.206 at Farnborough.*

U.K. DISTRIBUTORS: BEAS, OXFORD AIRPORT, KIDLINGTON, OXFORD. PHONE: KIDLINGTON 3363
OVERSEAS ENQUIRIES: BEAGLE AIRCRAFT LIMITED, REARSBY, LEICESTER, ENGLAND

BEAGLE AIRCRAFT LIMITED

Flight August 30th 1962
Ad Ref 39716

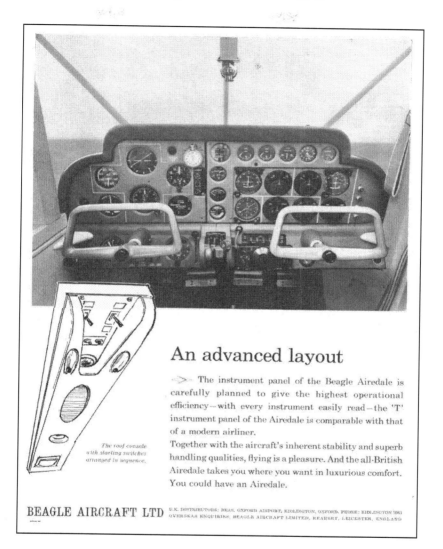

An advanced layout

> The instrument panel of the Beagle Airedale is carefully planned to give the highest operational efficiency—with every instrument easily read—the 'T' instrument panel of the Airedale is comparable with that of a modern airliner.

Together with the aircraft's inherent stability and superb handling qualities, flying is a pleasure. And the all-British Airedale takes you where you want in luxurious comfort. You could have an Airedale.

The roof console with starting switches arranged in sequence.

BEAGLE AIRCRAFT LTD U.K. DISTRIBUTORS: BEAS, OXFORD AIRPORT, KIDLINGTON, OXFORD. PHONE: KIDLINGTON 3061 OVERSEAS ENQUIRIES, BEAGLE AIRCRAFT LIMITED, REARSBY, LEICESTER, ENGLAND

Air Pictorial September 1962
Ad Ref 4164

Economy with Versatility

→ The Beagle Terrier 2 is a low-cost, robust two/three seat aircraft with a lively performance from its powerful de Havilland Gipsy Major 10 engine of 145 b.h.p. It is ideal for pleasure or leisure; touring and training; and makes a superb glider tug. Comfortable, colourful and easy to fly, dual control is standard and a blind flying panel is among the many optional extras available. The Terrier 2 is the ideal all-British, all-rounder — easy to own and easy to maintain. Available now at £2,195.

BEAGLE AIRCRAFT LIMITED U.K. DISTRIBUTOR: BEAS, OXFORD AIRPORT, KIDLINGTON, OXFORD. PHONE: KIDLINGTON 9363. OVERSEAS ENQUIRIES: BEAGLE AIRCRAFT LIMITED, REARSBY, LEICESTER, ENGLAND.

Air Pictorial October 1962
Ad Ref 4175

174

Beagle Aircraft 1960 - 1969

BEAS offer for immediate delivery
Two ex-demonstration de luxe Airedales.

G ARYZ. A superb model in blue and white with many luxury extras including: Long range tanks, Magnesyn Compass, Second Sensitive Altimeter and a Motorola M.135 Radio with V.O.R. It has flown only 125 hours and the current C. of A. expires in May 1963. Price £5,750.

G ARZR. Another luxury model in red and white, fitted with a King KX.100 radio with V.O.R. It has flown only 95 hours and the current C. of A. expires in May 1963. Price £5,400.

These aircraft and the new 1963 Airedale (available for demonstration) may be seen at Oxford Airport now.

FOR FURTHER DETAILS WRITE OR PHONE: BEAS, OXFORD AIRPORT, KIDLINGTON, OXFORD. PHONE: KIDLINGTON 3363.

Flight October 4th 1962
Ad Ref 39709

175

Aeroplane February 14th 1963
Ad Ref 39870

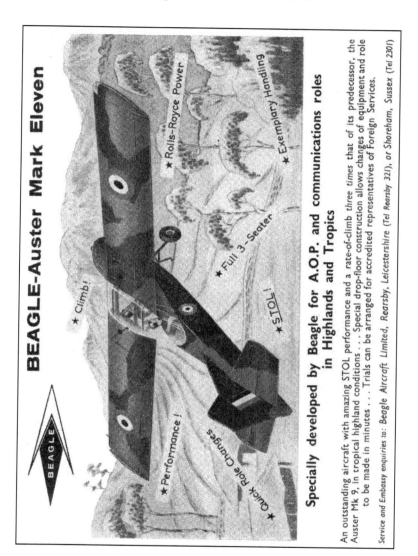

Flight February 21st 1963
Ad Ref 39855

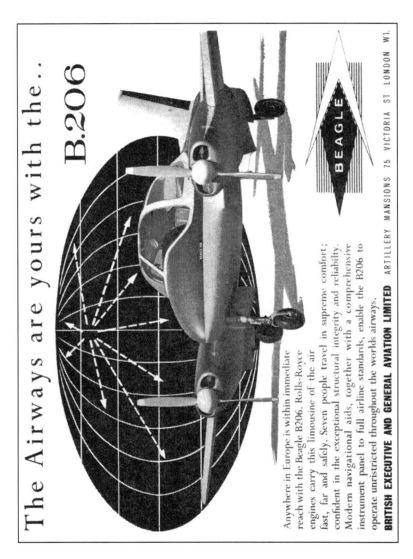

The Airways are yours with the..

B.206

Anywhere in Europe is within immediate reach with the Beagle B206. Rolls-Royce engines carry this limousine of the air fast, far and safely. Seven people travel in supreme comfort; confident in the exceptional structural integrity and reliability. Modern navigational aids, together with a comprehensive instrument panel to full airline standards, enable the B206 to operate unristricted throughout the worlds airways.

BRITISH EXECUTIVE AND GENERAL AVIATION LIMITED ARTILLERY MANSIONS 76 VICTORIA ST LONDON W1.

BEAGLE

Air Pictorial May 1963
Ad Ref 4196

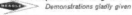
Aeroplane May 2nd 1963
Ad Ref 60935

Aeroplane July 25th 1963
Ad Ref 60936

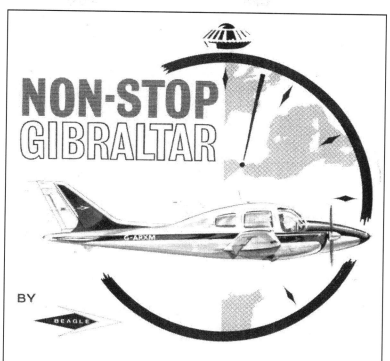

Flight August 29th 1963
Ad Ref 39871

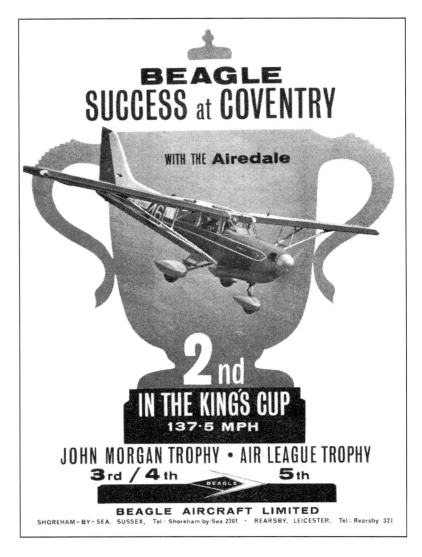

Flight September 12th 1963
Ad Ref 39874

Beagle Aircraft 1960 - 1969

The BEAGLE B.206 (two 310 h.p. Rolls-Royce Continental engines) is now in production for the Royal Air Force, the Ministry of Aviation and for civil customers. Deliveries will start early next year. This seven-seat "executive twin" recently demonstrated its qualities by flying non-stop from London to Gibraltar, 1,100 miles at 214 m.p.h. with full payload.

BEAGLE AIRCRAFT LIMITED
SHOREHAM AIRPORT · SHOREHAM-BY-SEA SUSSEX · TEL. 2301

Flight October 3rd 1963
Ad Ref 39873

Beagle Aircraft 1960 - 1969

Flight December 12th 1963
Ad Ref 39872

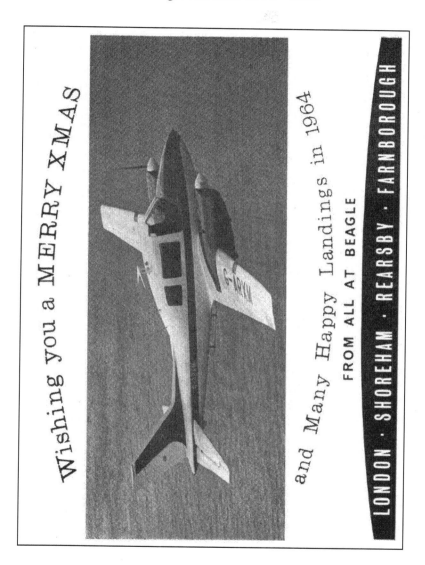

Wishing you a MERRY XMAS and Many Happy Landings in 1964

FROM ALL AT BEAGLE

LONDON · SHOREHAM · REARSBY · FARNBOROUGH

Flight December 19th 1963
Ad Ref 39875

Beagle Aircraft 1960 - 1969

Flight February 13th 1964
Ad Ref 40111

Beagle Aircraft 1960 - 1969

This is THE B206
POWERED BY ROLLS-ROYCE

For maximum utility, communications aircraft must be ready and waiting to transport passengers to distant appointments at a moment's notice. With this in mind, quick servicing and easy maintenance characteristics have been designed into the B.206. Emphasis on pleasant handling qualities and on airline standards of equipment for the pilot, and on width, comfort, ease of entry and airline amenities for the passenger enable the B.206 to provide fast, economical and dependable travel for civil and military users.

NOW IN QUANTITY PRODUCTION FOR CIVIL MARKETS AND FOR COMMUNICATIONS DUTIES WITH THE BRITISH ROYAL AIR FORCE

BETTER FLY BEAGLE

BEAGLE AIRCRAFT LIMITED
SHOREHAM AIRPORT SHOREHAM-BY-SEA SUSSEX TEL: 2301

Flight March 19th 1964
Ad Ref 40109

Flight May 21st 1964
Ad Ref 40112

Flight June 25th 1964
Ad Ref 40110

Fly *FIRST* Class
in your own limousine of the air

The BEAGLE
B.206

Fully equipped to fly
IN ALL WEATHERS –
IN ANY PART OF THE WORLD!

BEAGLE AIRCRAFT LIMITED
Rearsby Aerodrome Leicester Shoreham Airport Shoreham-by-Sea
TELEPHONE REARSBY 321   Sussex TELEPHONE 2301

Air Pictorial July 1964
Ad Ref 4844

Beagle Aircraft 1960 - 1969

Beagle's B.206 is the most modern and versatile light twin piston-engine military communications aircraft available in production for world markets.

Among its many outstanding characteristics are:

★ **EXCEPTIONALLY WIDE INSTRUMENT PANEL** (54 inches) making possible fully duplicated blind flying panels and full radio and navigational aids.

★ **SPECIAL ATTENTION** to layout of flight deck which meets I.A.T.A. and Transport Command requirements for transport aircraft.

★ **HYDRAULICALLY OPERATED AIR-STAIRS/BAGGAGE** door for ease of entrance and self-contained operation in the field.

★ **LARGE DOORS FOR ENTRANCE AND FREIGHT LOADING** to accommodate packages 56" × 40" × 31" (with loading ramp).

★ **STRONG FLOOR**—designed to accommodate loads of up to 250 lb. per sq. ft.

★ **FULLY DUPLICATED** electrical system.

★ **GUARANTEED FATIGUE LIFE** of 15,000 flying hours.

★ **DESIGN FOR MAINTENANCE** backed by provision of a full "exchange/overhaul" scheme for all components.

★ **FLEXIBILITY OF ROLES** which include:

Eight seats for 810 st. miles at 209 m.p.h.
Five seats with toilet for 1,600 st. miles at 209 m.p.h.

SEE US AT THE FARNBOROUGH AIR SHOW......
STAND J

BEAGLE

BEAGLE AIRCRAFT LIMITED

SHOREHAM AIRPORT, SHOREHAM-BY-SEA, SUSSEX. TELEPHONE: 2301.   REARSBY AERODROME, REARSBY, LEICESTERSHIRE. TELEPHONE: 321

Air Pictorial September 1964
Ad Ref 4836

Flight March 18th 1965
Ad Ref 40330

Beagle Aircraft 1960 - 1969

Flight April 22nd 1965
Ad Ref 40326

THE BEAGLE B206 ABOVE ALL

Now in full production in World Wide operation

Beagle leads with the B.206. Most modern, most versatile light twin piston-engine military communications aircraft available in production for world markets.

Among its many outstanding qualities:

* EXCEPTIONALLY WIDE INSTRUMENT PANEL (54 inches) making possible fully duplicated blind flying panels and full radio and navigational aids.

* SPECIAL ATTENTION to layout of flight deck which meets I.A.T.A. and Transport Command requirements for transport aircraft.

* HYDRAULICALLY OPERATED AIR-STAIRS/BAGGAGE door for ease of entrance and self-contained operation in the field.

* LARGE DOORS FOR ENTRANCE AND FREIGHT LOADING to accommodate packages 56" x 40" x 31" (with loading ramp).

* STRONG FLOOR—designed to accommodate loads of up to 250 lb. per sq. ft.

* FULLY DUPLICATED electrical system.

* GUARANTEED FATIGUE LIFE of 15,000 flying hours.

* DESIGN FOR MAINTENANCE backed by provision of a full 'exchange/overhaul' scheme for all components.

BEAGLE AIRCRAFT LIMITED SHOREHAM AIRPORT SHOREHAM-BY-SEA, SUSSEX. TELEPHONE 2301
REARSBY AERODROME, REARSBY, LEICESTERSHIRE. TELEPHONE 321

Aeroplane May 13th 1965
Ad Ref 60950

Flight May 13th 1965
Ad Ref 40328

Beagle Aircraft 1960 - 1969

THE BEAGLE B206 ABOVE ALL

Now in full production in World Wide operation

Beagle leads with the B.206. Most modern, most versatile light twin piston-engine military and civil communications aircraft available in production for world markets. Powered by Rolls-Royce

Among its many outstanding qualities:

* EXCEPTIONALLY WIDE INSTRUMENT PANEL (54 inches) making possible fully duplicated blind flying panels and full radio and navigational aids.
* SPECIAL ATTENTION to layout of flight deck which meets I.A.T.A and Transport Command requirements for transport aircraft.
* HYDRAULICALLY OPERATED AIR-STAIRS/BAGGAGE door for ease of entrance and self-contained operation in the field.
* LARGE DOORS FOR ENTRANCE AND FREIGHT LOADING to accommodate packages 56" x 40" x 31" (with loading ramp).
* STRONG FLOOR—designed to accommodate loads of up to 250 lb. per sq. ft.
* FULLY DUPLICATED electrical system.
* GUARANTEED FATIGUE LIFE of 15,000 flying hours.
* DESIGN FOR MAINTENANCE backed by provision of a full 'exchange/overhaul' scheme for all components.

 BEAGLE AIRCRAFT LIMITED SHOREHAM AIRPORT SHOREHAM-BY-SEA, SUSSEX. TELEPHONE 2301
REARSBY AERODROME, REARSBY, LEICESTERSHIRE. TELEPHONE 321

Flight June 10th 1965
Ad Ref 40327

196

Flight June 17th 1965
Ad Ref 40329

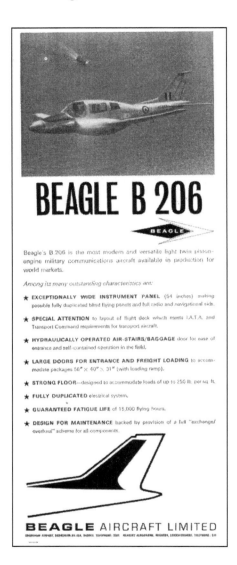

Air Pictorial September 1965
Ad Ref 4622

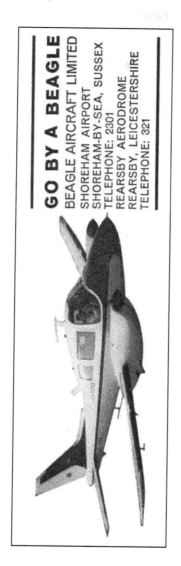

GO BY A BEAGLE

BEAGLE AIRCRAFT LIMITED
SHOREHAM AIRPORT
SHOREHAM-BY-SEA, SUSSEX
TELEPHONE: 2301
REARSBY AERODROME
REARSBY, LEICESTERSHIRE
TELEPHONE: 321

Flight September 23rd 1965
Ad Ref 40331

Air Pictorial November 1965
Ad Ref 4612

Air Pictorial March 1966
Ad Ref 4523

Beagle Aircraft 1960 - 1969

Flight March 10th 1966
Ad Ref 40711

BOOST
FOR THE BEAGLE

BEAGLE B.206-S

Now supercharged with continental engines supplied by Rolls-Royce

THE BEAGLE B.206-S provides a substantially enhanced high-altitude performance, for a relatively small increase in cost, by the use of two 340 h.p. Turbo-Supercharged Continental GTS10-520-C engines supplied by Rolls-Royce in place of the 310 h.p. engines in the B.206.

A summary of the chief performance characteristics follows:

■ Initial rate of climb: 1,340 ft./min. at 7,500 lb.

■ Take-off to 50 ft. in I.S.A. conditions, Sea Level, 10 knot wind at 7,500 lb.: 1,880 ft.

■ Cruising speed: 191 knots (220 m.p.h.) at 8,000 ft. (70% Max S.L. power).

■ Cruising speed: 191 knots (220 m.p.h.) at 12,000 ft. (65% Max S.L. power).

■ Maximum still air range: 1,400 nautical miles.

■ Maximum speed: 222 knots (255 m.p.h.) at 16,000 ft.

The B.206-S offers outstanding performance, under either temperate or tropical conditions for operation anywhere in the world and—like the B.206—it is backed with BEAGLE, Rolls-Royce and Continental after-sales service.

BEAGLE AIRCRAFT LIMITED   Shoreham Airport · Shoreham-by-Sea · Sussex · Telephone: 2301
Rearsby Aerodrome · Rearsby · Leicestershire · Telephone: 321

Flight June 23rd 1966
Ad Ref 40709

203

Air Pictorial September 1966
Ad Ref 4556

"Beagle is about to have Pups!

Come and see the first of the litter at Farnborough"

The new 100 h.p. Beagle "Pup" is an aerobatic two-seat
trainer with side-by-side seating and
occasional jump seat at rear. Designed for Private Owners
and Clubs. You can see the entire Beagle
range plus a special mock-up of the first Beagle "Pup"
on display at this year's Farnborough Air Show. **Stand J.**

For full details contact:
BEAGLE AIRCRAFT LIMITED
SHOREHAM AIRPORT · SHOREHAM-BY-SEA · SUSSEX · TELEPHONE: 2301
REARSBY AERODROME · REARSBY · LEICESTERSHIRE · TELEPHONE: 321

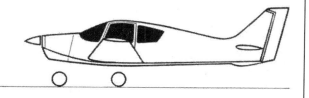

Flight September 8th 1966
Ad Ref 40712

Beagle B.206-S
Outstanding performance
plus luxury seating
for eight

The exceptionally wide cabin (62in) of the Beagle B.206-S makes possible first class airline standards of seating not normally found in aircraft of this category. With a total cabin volume of 221 cu. ft. (some 20 per cent greater than other contemporary aircraft in its class) the B.206-S is ideally suited for a variety of accommodation layouts for up to eight people. Powered by two 340 h.p. Turbo-Supercharged Continental GTSIO-520 engines supplied by Rolls-Royce.

CHIEF PERFORMANCE CHARACTERISTICS

Initial rate of climb: 1,340 ft/min. at 7,500 lb.
Take-off to 50 ft.
in I.S.A. Conditions, Sea Level, 10 knot wind at 7,500 lb; 1,880 ft.

Cruising speed:
191 knots (220 mph) at 8,000 ft. (70% Max. S. L. power).
Cruising speed:
191 knots (220 mph) at 12,000 ft. (65% Max. S. L. power).

Maximum still air range: 1,400 nautical miles.
Maximum speed: 222 knots (255 mph) at 16,000 ft.

For convenience . . . speed . . . economy of operation . . . it's the Beagle B.206-S above all.

BEAGLE AIRCRAFT LIMITED
Shoreham Airport · Shoreham-by-Sea · Sussex · Telephone: 2301
Rearsby Aerodrome · Rearsby · Leicestershire · Telephone: 321

Air Pictorial November 1966
Ad Ref 4540

Flight December 1st 1966
Ad Ref 40708

Flight December 15th 1966
Ad Ref 40710

top companies fly Beagle

right to the far corners of the world

...BECAUSE BEAGLE IS THE BEST BUY-IN 6-8 SEAT EXECUTIVE AIRCRAFT

☐ Has the longest range : 1,400 nautical miles.
☐ Has the largest door, behind the wing, for passengers and freight.
☐ Has the quietest passenger compartment, the largest windows
with the best view.
☐ Has the largest and most comfortable seats.
☐ Has outstanding stability, most pleasant flying characteristics
and a separate crew compartment.
☐ Has all-weather capability, including full de-icing.
☐ is equipped to full airline standards of radio, navigational
aids and coupled auto-pilot.
☐ Has turbo-supercharged Continental engines supplied by Rolls-Royce.
☐ Has fast, efficient spares and maintenance service.
☐ Has the most robust construction for long operational life.
☐ Is British, built in Britain.

*Rolls-Royce and the Imperial Tobacco Company are two of the top
British Companies who are now Beagling their way to better business.*

BEAGLE AIRCRAFT LIMITED
Shoreham Airport, Shoreham-by-Sea, Sussex. Telephone: 2301
Rearsby Aerodrome, Rearsby, Leicestershire. Telephone: 321

Flying Review January 1967
Ad Ref 40956

Beagle Aircraft 1960 - 1969

Flight February 23rd 1967
Ad Ref 61030

Flight March 16th 1967
Ad Ref 40951

wait for it!!

If you're thinking of buying a new light aeroplane, don't—until you know more about the Beagle Pup. It will be launched later in the year. Cost, £3,495 basic. Range, up to 500 miles. Engine, the tested and proved Rolls-Royce Continental. Plus, the proved British know-how of Beagle Aircraft. Interested? Then fill in the coupon.

Post to: BEAGLE AIRCRAFT LIMITED, Shoreham Airport, Shoreham-by-sea, Sussex
Please send me (without obligation) all the details about the Beagle Pup.

NAME

ADDRESS

Flight March 30th 1967
Ad Ref 40958

Beagle Aircraft 1960 - 1969

Flight April 20th 1967
Ad Ref 40945

Flight April 27th 1967
Ad Ref 40946

ease of access

*No clambering over the wing to board the B.206-S. A large
upward opening door with a simple 'three step' pull-down air stair
gives the Beagle B.206-S ease of access, even for a lady in a tight skirt.
Door measurements are 40" high by 34" wide—easy loading of large crates and
packages when the aircraft is used in a cargo carrying role.*

This and nine other reasons make the Beagle B.206-S the World's 'best buy' in 6/8 seat passenger aircraft.

1. Has a long range of 1,400 nautical miles. **2.** The quietest passenger compartment, the largest windows with the best
views. **3.** The largest and most comfortable seats. **4.** Outstanding stability, most pleasant flying characteristics and a
separate crew compartment. **5.** All-weather capability including full de-icing. **6.** Is equipped to full airline standards
of radio, navigational aids and coupled auto-pilot. **7.** Turbo-supercharged Continental engines supplied by
Rolls-Royce. **8.** Fast, efficient spares and maintenance service. **9.** Has the most robust construction for long
operational life. Is British, built in Britain.

*Beagle Aircraft Ltd., Shoreham Airport, Shoreham-by-Sea, Sussex. Telephone: Shoreham 2301
Rearsby Aerodrome, Rearsby, Leicestershire. Telephone: Rearsby 321*

Air Pictorial May 1967
Ad Ref 4382

Putting the Pup through its paces

April 8th, 1967. Pup makes its first flight at Shoreham.

The Pup project's off the ground

Well up to schedule—that's the progress report on the Beagle Pup. When it first flew at Shoreham, it opened a new era in club flying. For from nose to tail, the Pup is designed as something more than another light aeroplane—it's the start of a whole new concept.

For instance, the styling. It's as elegant as a modern sports car. The cabin is exceptionally roomy and luxurious, the controls simply and clearly placed. Two doors help to make access easy. The Pup isn't just

beautiful, it's also strong as a horse, with corrosion protection on *all* interior structures. The Pup has many other advanced features too, which you'll find on very few other light aircraft.

Add to all this real economy, ease of servicing, long life, low fuel consumption (22 mpg) a range in excess of 500 miles, aerobatic handling—and you have the most advanced, most sophisticated light aircraft in the World ... at £3,495, it will be easily the best value for money.

Beagle Aircraft Limited Shoreham Airport, Shoreham-by-sea, Sussex. Telephone: 2301
Rearsby Aerodrome, Rearsby, Leicestershire. Telephone: 321

Flight May 11th 1967
Ad Ref 40959

Flight May 25th 1967
Ad Ref 40960

Putting the Pup through its paces

The Pup is by far the most comfortable light aircraft

Take a good look at the cabin of the Pup, and you will be impressed by what you see. Here is nothing less than a whole new concept in club flying. For instance, there are two doors to give easy access. Not only are the seats comfortable—they're really luxurious. And the instrument panel is arranged with the basic 'T'. Other instruments are arranged in a neat and logical order. The hydraulic brakes are toe-operated. Add to this air ventilating and heating like a car, with all of four inches more elbow room than any comparable aeroplane, and the connoisseurs clearly have very good reason for their enthusiasm. But the Pup is a great deal more than elegant and intelligent. It's strong, with inner corrosion protection on *all* interior structures. Refinements include electrically operated flaps, and ball bearings at all control pivots. Oleo pneumatic suspension on all three wheels makes servicing far easier and simpler—and all maintenance is from outside the aeroplane. To these outstanding points you can also add a remarkable stinginess with fuel—all of 22 mpg and a range of 500 miles. In short, what we're making, and what those who use them will appreciate, is the most advanced, most sophisticated light aircraft in the World today . . . and at £3,495 really good value for money.

Beagle Aircraft Limited, Shoreham Airport, Shoreham-by-Sea, Sussex. Telephone: 2301
Rearsby Aerodrome, Rearsby, Leicestershire. Telephone : 321

Air Pictorial July 1967
Ad Ref 4406

The outstanding new Beagle Pup
will be ready for delivery early 1968. For £3,495.
It will cruise at 120 m.p.h., give 500 miles
at 22 m.p.g., have a Rolls-Royce engine, two
doors for easy access, electrically operated
flaps, ball bearing control pivots, three
wheel oleo-pneumatic suspension, inner
corrosion protection on all structures, a
wider, sumptuously appointed cabin, can be
maintained from the outside only, and
performs aerobatically on an economical
100 h.p. . . .

. . . Otherwise it's no different
from ordinary light aircraft

Flying Review July 1967
Ad Ref 40962

Rolls-Royce expect a lot from their executive aircraft. They get it from the BEAGLE B.206

Rolls-Royce took delivery of their Beagle on the 25th May 1965. Since then it has stacked thousands of air miles. It has flown to a great many places in Italy, Switzerland and France, and throughout the U.K. Rolls-Royce work their aircraft hard and often. That's why they ordered a Beagle, because it has *proved* reliability.

These reasons make the Beagle B.206 the world's 'best buy' in 6-8 seat passenger aircraft. 1. Has a range of 1,400 miles. 2. A quiet passenger compartment with really large windows. 3. Large and comfortable seats. 4. Outstanding stability, most pleasant flying characteristics and a separate crew compartment. 5. All-weather capability, including full de-icing. 6. Is equipped to full airline standards of radio, navigational aids and coupled auto-pilot. 7. Continental engines supplied by Rolls-Royce. 8. Fast, efficient spares and maintenance service. 9. Has the most robust construction for long operational life. In addition, the latest version of this aircraft, the B.206-S is fitted with turbo supercharged Continental engines supplied by Rolls-Royce, and has a large door behind the wing for passengers and cargo. Is British, built in Britain.

Beagle

Beagle Aircraft Limited,
Shoreham Airport, Shoreham-by-Sea, Sussex. Tel : Shoreham 2301.
Rearsby Aerodrome, Rearsby, Leicestershire. Telephone : Rearsby 321.

Air Pictorial August 1967
Ad Ref 4408

Flying Review August 1967
Ad Ref 40961

Complete structural integrity – tested to transport aircraft standards – gives the B.206-S a guaranteed fatigue life of 15,000 hours, the longest of any aircraft in its class.

The *Beagle* B.206-S is good and strong

Flight August 3rd 1967
Ad Ref 40947

Flight August 31st 1967
Ad Ref 40948

Air Pictorial September 1967
Ad Ref 4411

Beagle Aircraft 1960 - 1969

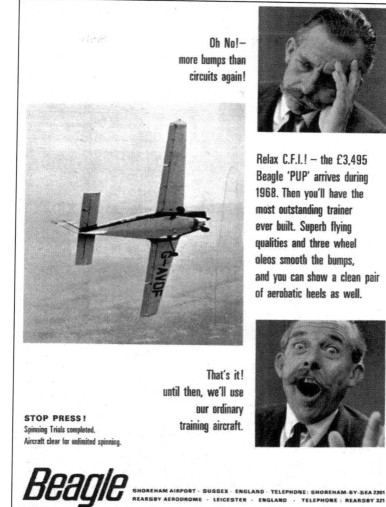

Oh No!–
more bumps than
circuits again!

Relax C.F.I.! – the £3,495
Beagle 'PUP' arrives during
1968. Then you'll have the
most outstanding trainer
ever built. Superb flying
qualities and three wheel
oleos smooth the bumps,
and you can show a clean pair
of aerobatic heels as well.

That's it!
until then, we'll use
our ordinary
training aircraft.

STOP PRESS!
Spinning Trials completed.
Aircraft clear for unlimited spinning.

Beagle
SHOREHAM AIRPORT · SUSSEX · ENGLAND · TELEPHONE: SHOREHAM-BY-SEA 2301
REARSBY AERODROME · LEICESTER · ENGLAND · TELEPHONE: REARSBY 321

Flying Review September 1967
Ad Ref 40964

Beagle Aircraft 1960 - 1969

Flight September 21st 1967
Ad Ref 40957

Beagle Aircraft 1960 - 1969

The *Beagle* B.206-S has a good and quiet cabin

Efficient sound proofing, including double-glazed windows make the B.206-S the quietest aircraft of its class.

Flight October 19th 1967
Ad Ref 40955

227

Love to fly
old boy!
Too expensive
for me though!

Not so in the new Beagle 'PUP'
the economical 100 h.p. Rolls Royce
engine and high performance
airframe, gives 500 miles at 22
m.p.g. Easy access panels, non-
lubricated bearings, inter-
changeable parts, and a superb
spares service, cuts flying costs.

That's more like it!
I seriously think
I could have a go!

STOP PRESS!
Spinning Trials completed.
Tropical Trials successful.

SHOREHAM AIRPORT · SUSSEX · ENGLAND · TELEPHONE: SHOREHAM-BY-SEA 2301
REARSBY AERODROME · LEICESTER · ENGLAND · TELEPHONE: REARSBY 321

Flying Review November 1967
Ad Ref 40963

Flight November 9th 1967
Ad Ref 40953

Beagle Aircraft 1960 - 1969

Flight November 16th 1967
Ad Ref 40954

230

Yet another top company selects Beagle

Time flies quickly at GKN, so now it's the *direct route with the B.206-S

Do YOU have time to spare?

* the GKN Group has over 120 operating units throughout the United Kingdom and interests in many European countries. Their Beagle is well employed.

Beagle Aircraft Limited,
Shoreham Airport, Shoreham-by-Sea, Sussex. Tel : Shoreham 2301
Rearsby Aerodrome, Rearsby, Leicestershire. Telephone : Rearsby 321

Flight November 23rd 1967
Ad Ref 40952

Air Pictorial December 1967
Ad Ref 4428

Beagle Aircraft 1960 - 1969

Flight December 21st 1967
Ad Ref 40949

Flying Doctors switch to Beagle.

Operating out of the mining community of Broken Hill and covering a territory of 309,460 square miles, the New South Wales Division of the Royal Australian Flying Doctors Service has switched from specially built three-engine aircraft to standard Beagle B.206-S twins. The first aircraft have already been delivered (flying halfway round the world to get there) and others are on order to complete the change-over. Why have the Flying Doctors chosen Beagle?

LONG DISTANCES, HIGH TEMPERATURES, SHORT DESTRUCTIVE AIRSTRIPS

The primary reason is that the Beagles will have to operate in conditions of utmost severity. They will have to log thousands of miles in daily routine doctors' rounds (only one in fifty trips is the dramatic emergency dash of fiction), flying in temperatures which can rocket as high as 115°F and then drop as suddenly, working from destructively bumpy home-made airstrips amongst the scrub and porcupine grass.

When that fiftieth call happens, and there is an emergency, it may demand an aircraft to race as much as 700 miles clear across the State and send it dodging amongst mountains more than 6,000 ft. high in the coastal ranges.

The Beagle can do all this effortlessly. It has an immensely strong airframe which has been tested for both static strength and fatigue endurance far beyond normal limits. Duplicated systems, duplicated load paths and what FLIGHT INTERNATIONAL calls 'an extraordinary degree of structural continuity' give it the robustness and reliability of a small airliner.

Turbo-supercharged 340 hp Continental engines supplied by Rolls-Royce provide sparkling high altitude performance, in 'hot and high' airfield conditions and a tropical climate. The Beagle B.206-S can climb at 1,340 ft/min, can cruise at 220 mph and has a range of 1,400 miles.

It has also been designed for fast and easy servicing and has the backing of the World-wide after sales service of Beagle and Rolls-Royce behind it.

COMFORT, SILENCE AND SPACE FOR THE SICK, INJURED OR PREGNANT

Another reason for the New South Wales doctors' choice is that patients need comfort and the Beagle provides it. The large cabin (62" wide and 131" long) which normally provides first class airline accommodation for six or eight passengers makes the Beagle a perfect air ambulance.

The optional bulkhead which can turn the cabin into a private conference room is replaced in this case by a storage unit for medical supplies and instruments. The big door behind the wing (it measures 40" deep by 34" wide) gives exceptionally easy access for both stretchers and walking patients. The outstanding soundproofing makes the Beagle B.206-S a very quiet and therefore restful aircraft.

ALL-WEATHER PERFORMANCE

Finally, the Beagle B.206-S is an all-weather aircraft with full de-icing, is equipped to full airline standards of radio, navigational aids and coupled auto-pilot, and is available with a complete range of optional additional equipment. It is also exceptionally stable and pleasant to fly.

The characteristics that make it the best choice for New South Wales' Flying Doctors make it the best buy in 6-8 seat aircraft. Shouldn't your company be considering a B.206-S?

BEAGLE AIRCRAFT LIMITED
Shoreham Airport, Shoreham-by-Sea, Sussex. Tel: Shoreham 2301
Rearsby Aerodrome, Rearsby, Leicestershire. Tel: Rearsby 321

Broken Hill. The Royal Flying Doctor Service Radio Base in N.S.W.

c

Flight January 25th 1968
Ad Ref 41217

Air Pictorial February 1968
Ad Ref 4715

Yet another top company selects Beagle

Time flies quickly at GKN, so now it's the *direct route with the B.206-S

Do YOU have time to spare?

* the GKN Group has over 120 operating units throughout the United Kingdom and interests in many European countries. Their Beagle is well employed.

Beagle Aircraft Limited,
Shoreham Airport, Shoreham-by-Sea, Sussex. Tel: Shoreham 2301
Rearsby Aerodrome, Rearsby, Leicestershire. Telephone: Rearsby 321

Flight February 29th 1968
Ad Ref 41220

236

Beagle Aircraft 1960 - 1969

For Business or pleasure

it's better by *Beagle*

The superb Beagle 206-S, the last word in eight-seat executive aircraft, "Tops" in structural integrity, quiet comfort, performance, and unbeatable value for money. Ask now for free evaluation and demonstration for your company. Also, the great new Beagle "Pup" range of training and sporting aircraft. *Send for details today.*

BEAGLE AIRCRAFT LTD., Shoreham Airport, Sussex, England : Telephone: Shoreham-by-Sea 2301
Rearsby Aerodrome, Leicester, England : Telephone: Rearsby 321

Flight April 25th 1968
Ad Ref 41219

237

Beagle Aircraft 1960 - 1969

For Business or pleasure

it's better by Beagle

The superb Beagle 206-S, the last word in eight-seat executive aircraft, "Tops" in structural integrity, quiet comfort, performance, and unbeatable value for money. Ask now for free evaluation and demonstration for your company. Also, the great new Beagle "Pup" range of training and sporting aircraft. *Send for details today.*

 AIRCRAFT LTD

SHOREHAM AIRPORT · SUSSEX · ENGLAND · TELEPHONE: SHOREHAM-BY-SEA 2301

REARSBY AERODROME · LEICESTER · ENGLAND · TELEPHONE: REARSBY 321

Air Pictorial June 1968
Ad Ref 4733

Beagle Aircraft 1960 - 1969

For Business
or pleasure
it's better by Beagle

Flying Review June 1968
Ad Ref 41221

239

Flight August 15th 1968
Ad Ref 41222

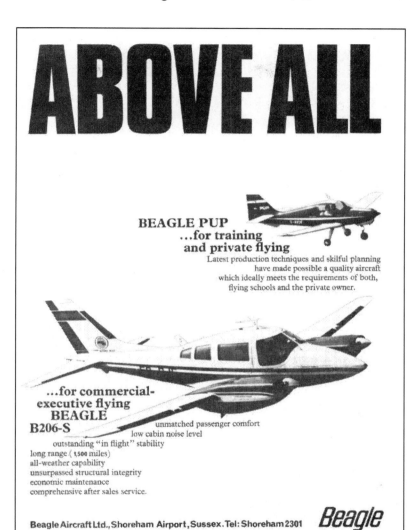

Flight September 26th 1968
Ad Ref 41218

Flying Review December 1968
Ad Ref 41223

Beagle Aircraft 1960 - 1969

For Business
or pleasure
it's better by Beagle

The superb Beagle 206-S, the last word in eight-seat executive aircraft, "Tops" in structural integrity, quiet comfort, performance, and unbeatable value for money. Ask now for free evaluation and demonstration for your company. Also, the great new Beagle "Pup" range of training and sporting aircraft. *Send for details today.*

AIRCRAFT LTD

SHOREHAM AIRPORT   SUSSEX   ENGLAND   TELEPHONE: SHOREHAM-BY-SEA 2301

REARSBY AERODROME   LEICESTER   ENGLAND   TELEPHONE: REARSBY 321

Flight January 23rd 1969
Ad Ref 41470

Beagle Aircraft 1960 - 1969

For Business or pleasure it's better by Beagle

Beagle Aircraft Ltd., Shoreham Airport, Sussex. Tel: Shoreham 2301   *Beagle*

Flight April 24th 1969
Ad Ref 41469

244

Flying Review April 1969
Ad Ref 41472

Flight August 28th 1969
Ad Ref 45110

BEAGLE
are building B206-S's Pup-100's Pup-150's and Bulldogs for World Markets. All are selling well.

Beagle Aircraft Limited
Shoreham Airport
Sussex BN4 5FJ
England.

Flight September 4th 1969
Ad Ref 41471

Congratulations

to

Peter Clifford Aviation Ltd

and

Truman Aviation Ltd

on selling more than

90 PUPS

in Britain during the past twelve months

Beagle Aircraft Ltd Shoreham Airport Sussex BN4 5FJ
Tel: Shoreham-by-Sea 2301

Peter Clifford Aviation Ltd
White Waltham Airfield
Nr. Maidenhead, Berks
Tel: Littlewick Green 3341

Truman Aviation Ltd
Huntingdon Street
Nottingham NG1 3NJ
Tel: Nottingham 52881

Air Pictorial September 1969
Ad Ref 4931

The Bulldog

Scottish Aviation Ltd
British Aerospace plc. BAe

bulldog -

designed for effect

The Scottish Aviation BULLDOG is the most effective basic trainer available today. It will happily perform the most demanding Air Force training operations and will readily achieve intensive large Civilian Training School schedules. The *fully* aerobatic BULLDOG will operate effectively in the following roles ···

Basic Flying Training

Instrument Flying

Radio Navigation and Airways Training

Sports Flying and Touring

Glider Towing

Military Liaison and Observation

Weapon Training and Light Strike

Supply Dropping.

Precise and beautifully harmonised controls make BULLDOG flying a pleasure. The brisk climb and lively general performance fit well into the the basic Training School pattern and the tough tested airframe is stressed to plus 6G and minus 3G. The big cabin will accommodate big pilots with full emergency kit and the comprehensive standard specification includes a blind flying panel, dual controls and brakes, a spacious instrument panel,

jettisonable sliding canopy and a simply managed fuel system. With the addition of avionics the standard BULLDOG Series 100 is operationally complete. The proven 200 h.p. Avco Lycoming engine and easy maintenance ensures reliability for high utilisation.

the bulldog effect is to train effectively

Scottish Aviation Limited, Prestwick Airport, Scotland.

Flight June 10th 1971
Ad Ref 56894

250

The Bulldog 1969 - 1978

The plane truth.

You'll see a grand parade of aircraft at Farnborough-Europe '72. The giants of tomorrow . . . like Concorde. Soon to carry passengers at twice the speed of sound . . . TriStar, flying so quietly on its Rolls-Royce engines that herald a new silence in the skies. Progress to revolutionise air transport. Aircraft to steal the limelight of the jet age.

But Air transport isn't all big multi-seat airliners. There's a need around the world for commuter aircraft to serve the lesser air routes, for luxury planes to carry executives smoothly, speedily, to the Board Room; for rugged basic trainers to school the new generation of military pilots, and flying classrooms to provide experience in special skills.

You may have to search among the giants at Farnborough to find our sleek Jetstream and versatile Bulldog. But they're worth looking for. Proven machines matching reliability with economy in operation. Offered at prices competitive in world markets. A vital part of the British Aviation Industry's success story.

The Scottish Aviation Jetstream—
Business Aircraft— Feeder Liner.

The Scottish Aviation Bulldog—Military Basic Trainer

Jetstream and Bulldog. Scottish Aviation are producing both in quantity now. The RAF have ordered 26 Jetstreams. And various European, African and Asian Air Forces have already spoken for 228 Bulldog military trainers. Of course, this is all very nice, but we are a lot more than brilliant air-craft-makers. We have a lot more to offer. See how much more on Stand No. 15, Farnborough Air Show.

SCOTTISH AVIATION LIMITED. STAND Nº15
A member of The Laird Group. Prestwick International Airport. Scotland.

Air Pictorial September 1972
Ad Ref 5064

251

The Bulldog 1969 - 1978

Scottish Aviation climbing high -with the Bulldog

The Bulldog will become a classic. This opinion comes, not from Scottish Aviation, but from independent aviation experts. It will be a classic aircraft because it fulfils completely its role as a tough military basic trainer. Quality control is meticulous. The design guarantees efficiency and reliability. The Bulldog is now being produced in quantity by Scottish Aviation who have drawn upon their 37 years of experience combined with every modern facility not only to produce the aircraft, but to provide the "after sales service" required by today's Air Forces.

The Bulldog Military Basic Trainer is fully aerobatic and will perform the most demanding Air Force training operations. It can carry comprehensive instrumentation and avionics and is already being delivered to Air Forces in Europe, Africa and Asia.
So the Bulldog is aptly named. It is tough, reliable and exactly right for the job it has been carefully designed to do. These qualities make it a leader. And the Bulldog's lead is firmly held by Scottish Aviation, who are now climbing higher than ever. Right to the top, in fact.

Scottish Aviation Limited,
Prestwick International Airport, Scotland.

Flight December 7th 1972
Ad Ref 57086

The Bulldog 1969 - 1978

Flight May 24th 1973
Ad Ref 57324

253

Air Pictorial June 1973
Ad Ref 5163

Flight January 24th 1974
Ad Ref 57579

Air Pictorial September 1974
Ad Ref 1592

The Bulldog 1969 - 1978

Flight August 28th 1975
Ad Ref 57937

Flight September 4th 1976
Ad Ref 58193

The Bulldog 1969 - 1978

Over 250 Aerobatic Bulldogs are now in service world-wide - training more pilots in basic military flying skills than any competitor

Flight September 4th 1976
Ad Ref 58194

The Bulldog 1969 - 1978

Air Pictorial September 1977
Ad Ref 5254

260

Air Pictorial February 1978
Ad Ref 5309

Over 250 Aerobatic Bulldogs are now in service world-wide-
training more pilots in basic military flying skills than any competitor

BRITISH AEROSPACE
AIRCRAFT GROUP
SCOTTISH DIVISION
PRESTWICK AIRPORT, SCOTLAND
Tel 0292 79888 Telex 77432

Bulldogs have won approval and acceptance from 11 operators in 9 nations. Already, military and civil training organisations have placed repeat orders having proved that Bulldog shapes not only skills in technique, but a pilot's whole attitude to flying.

Superb flying qualities and sound engineering features backed by a continuous development programme and proven product support service combine to offer today's most reliable and cost-effective military light aircraft. The current Production Series 120 Bulldog embodies all the experience gained from 250,000 flying hours accumulated by aircraft in operational service

Bulldog's wide operational scope can be further extended, for light-strike, weapons training, supply dropping, liaison, reconnaissance, or patrol roles.

Flight March 4th 1978
Ad Ref 59036

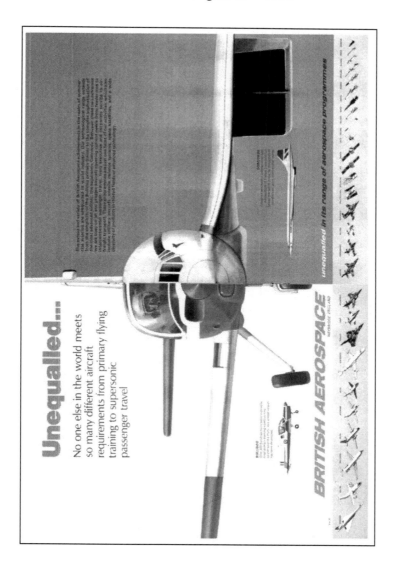

Flight October 28th 1978
Ad Ref 58943

Air Pictorial November 1978
Ad Ref 5307

The Bulldog 1969 - 1978

Flight November 25th 1978
Ad Ref 58946

265

Extras
Associated Engines

The *dependable* GIPSY goes into front-line action

The Taylorcraft Auster III Artillery Observation Aircraft —now in the spearhead of the attack—is powered by the de Havilland Gipsy Major Series I Engine.

DE HAVILLAND GIPSY ENGINES

Flight October 28th 1943
Ad Ref 27211

For reliability over the
front line the Taylorcraft
AUSTER III
artillery fire spotter is
powered by the de Havilland
Gipsy Major engine

DE HAVILLAND ENGINES
In the attack to-day — on the trade routes of the future

Aeroplane April 21st 1944
Ad Ref 27486

GIPSY *Proven* RELIABILITY

for the aircraft of to-day

The Auster Avis four-place personal aircraft
powered by a de Havilland Gipsy Major 10
four-cylinder engine of 145 b.h.p.

DE HAVILLAND

GIPSY ENGINES

Flight August 5th 1948
Ad Ref 28313

Aeronautics September 1949
Ad Ref 61419

Flight August 24th 1961
Ad Ref 15887

ROLLS-ROYCE
proven power for
LIGHT AIRCRAFT

Rolls-Royce offers operators of Continental light aircraft engines a factory repair and overhaul service, a comprehensive stock of spare parts, and the facilities of a European network of distributors. All current models of Continental engines (65-390 b.h.p.) can be supplied, and selected engines of Rolls-Royce manufacture will be available during 1962. Continental engines power more than 50,000 of the world's light aircraft and have flown many millions of miles.

Details may be obtained from the

LIGHT AIRCRAFT ENGINE DEPARTMENT · ROLLS-ROYCE LIMITED · CREWE

Aeroplane April 12th 1962
Ad Ref 60926

ROLLS-ROYCE
POWER FOR THE
BEAGLE 218 AND BEAGLE 206 AIRCRAFT

The Beagle 218 is powered by two 0-300-E engines each of 145 h.p. and the Beagle 206 by two GIO-470-E engines each of 310 h.p. These and other Continental light aircraft engines are being manufactured under licence by Rolls-Royce. The extensive overhaul and spares facilities at Crewe ensure prompt service to all operators of Continental engines.

ROLLS-ROYCE *Continental* PISTON ENGINES

ROLLS-ROYCE LIMITED, LIGHT AIRCRAFT ENGINE DEPARTMENT, CREWE.
ROLLS-ROYCE — AERO ENGINES · MOTOR CARS · DIESEL AND PETROL ENGINES · ROCKET MOTORS · NUCLEAR PROPULSION

Aeroplane September 13th 1962
Ad Ref 39842

Air Pictorial May 1975
Ad Ref 1616

For details of new catalogues in the series please visit
www.aviationancestry.co.uk